WEBSTER AND HAYNE'S
SPEECHES

WEBSTER AND HAYNE'S SPEECHES

IN THE UNITED STATES SENATE,

ON

MR. FOOT'S RESOLUTION OF JANUARY, 1830.

ALSO,

DANIEL WEBSTER'S SPEECH,

IN THE UNITED STATES SENATE, MARCH 7, 1850,

ON THE SLAVERY COMPROMISE.

"When my eyes shall be turned to behold, for the last time, the sun in heaven, may I not see him shining on the broken and dishonored fragments of a once glorious Union; on States dissevered, discordant, belligerent; on a land rent with civil feuds, or drenched, it may be, in fraternal blood! Let their last feeble and lingering glance, rather, behold the glorious ensign of the republic, now known and honored throughout the earth, still full high advanced, its arms and trophies streaming in their original lustre, not a stripe erased or polluted, nor a single star obscured, bearing for its motto no such miserable words of delusion and folly, as *'Liberty first, and Union afterwards;'* but everywhere, spread all over in characters of living light, blazing on all its ample folds, as they float over the sea and over the land, and in every wind under the whole heavens, that other sentiment dear to every true American heart— *'Liberty and Union, now and forever, one and inseparable!'* "—*Daniel Webster.*

The Black Heritage Library Collection

BOOKS FOR LIBRARIES PRESS
FREEPORT, NEW YORK
1971

First Published 1850
Reprinted 1971

E381
W 372

Reprinted from a copy in the
Fisk University Library Negro Collection

INTERNATIONAL STANDARD BOOK NUMBER:
0-8369-8955-4

LIBRARY OF CONGRESS CATALOG CARD NUMBER:
71-37318

PRINTED IN THE UNITED STATES OF AMERICA
BY
NEW WORLD BOOK MANUFACTURING CO., INC.
HALLANDALE, FLORIDA 33009

PREFACE.

ONE or two preliminary remarks upon the establishment of the administrations of 1825 and 1829 may render some of the allusions in these speeches more intelligible to those readers who are not familiar with the political history of the day.

The election of a President of the United States for the term beginning March 4, 1825, devolved upon the House of Representatives. The whole electoral vote was 261 — of which Andrew Jackson had 99, John Quincy Adams 84, William H. Crawford 41, and Henry Clay 37. The house, by the constitution, was limited to the first three in making a choice, and the vote was by states. Until the election actually took place, there was much doubt as to the result, but on the first ballot Adams received the votes of thirteen states, Jackson seven, and Crawford four; and Adams was thus elected. The vote was so close, however, that a rumor was put in circulation of a corrupt understanding between Adams and Clay, by which the friends of the latter, who was not a constitutional candidate, voted for Adams, in consideration of the bestowal of the office of secretary of state upon Clay by Adams in forming his cabinet. This calumny was disproved by all the testimony which could be brought to bear upon a negative proposition; and although at present it is probably not credited by any body, the suspicion of such a "coalition" seriously affected the popularity of both Adams and Clay at the time, and Colonel Hayne in his speech alluded to it, intimating that Webster had hopes of the office of secretary of state himself, which were frustrated by the appointment of Clay.

At the next presidential election, that of 1828, Adams and Jackson were opposing candidates, and the latter was chosen by a large popular majority. This result was brought about by the active coöperation with Jackson's original supporters of the friends of Mr. Calhoun and many of the friends of the other candidates of 1824. This coöperation implied the combination of the most discordant materials. The friends of Calhoun generally gave their aid, in the expectation that their favorite would be the next candidate, and in this way would receive the support of Jackson's other present supporters. How unfounded was any such expectation was proved by the actual result, by which Jackson was elected for a second term, and after him Van Buren, Calhoun being entirely neglected. It was in prophecy of this result that Mr. Webster quoted Shakspeare to the Vice President, Calhoun, reminding him that those who had foully removed Banquo had placed

> " A barren seeptre in their gripe,
> Thence to be wrenched by an unlineal hand,
> No son of theirs succeeding."

Although at the time of the speech there was the most perfect cordiality between Jackscn and Calhoun and their friends and supporters.

155063

MR. HAYNE'S SPEECH.

Debate in the Senate on Mr. Foot's Resolution, Thursday, January 21, 1830.

Mr. Foot's resolution being under consideration, —

[When Mr. Webster concluded his first speech on Wednesday, the 20th, Mr. Benton followed with some remarks in reply to Mr. W., but as they were principally embodied in his more extended speech some days after, those remarks are omitted. On the day following, Mr. Hayne took the floor in the following rejoinder to Mr. Webster.]

Mr. HAYNE said, when he took occasion, two days ago, to throw out some ideas with respect to the policy of the government, in relation to the public lands, nothing certainly could have been further from his thoughts, than that he should have been compelled again to throw himself upon the indulgence of the Senate. Little did I expect, said Mr. H., to be called upon to meet such an argument as was yesterday urged by the gentleman from Massachusetts, (Mr. Webster.) Sir, I questioned no man's opinions; I impeached no man's motives; I charged no party, or state, or section of country with hostility to any other, but ventured, as I thought, in a becoming spirit, to put forth my own sentiments in relation to a great national question of public policy. Such was my course. The gentleman from Missouri, (Mr. Benton,) it is true, had charged upon the Eastern States an early and continued hostility towards the west, and referred to a number of historical facts and documents in support of that charge. Now, sir, how have these different arguments been met? The honorable gentleman from Massachusetts, after deliberating a whole night upon his course, comes into this chamber to vindicate New England; and instead of making up his issue with the gentleman from Missouri, on the charges which *he had preferred*, chooses to consider me as the author of those charges, and losing sight entirely of that gentleman, selects me as his adversary, and pours out all the vials of his mighty wrath upon my devoted head. Nor is he willing to stop there. He goes on to assail the institutions and policy of the south, and calls in question the principles and conduct of the state which I have the honor to represent. When I find a gentleman of mature age and experience, of acknowledged talents and profound sagacity, pursuing a course like this, declining the contest offered from the west, and making war upon the unoffending south, I must believe, I am bound to believe, he has some object in view which he has not ventured to disclose. Mr. President, why is this? Has the gentleman discovered in former controversies with the gentleman from Missouri, that he is overmatched by that senator? And does he hope for an easy victory over a more feeble adversary? Has the gentleman's distempered fancy been disturbed by gloomy forebodings of "new alliances to be formed," at which he hinted? Has the ghost of the

murdered COALITION come back, like the ghost of Banquo, to "sear the
eyeballs of the gentleman," and will it not down at his bidding? Are
dark visions of broken hopes, and honors lost forever, still floating before
his heated imagination? Sir, if it be his object to thrust me between the
gentleman from Missouri and himself, in order to rescue the east from the
contest it has provoked with the west, he shall not be gratified. Sir, I
will not be dragged into the defence of my friend from Missouri. The
south shall not be forced into a conflict not its own. The gentleman from
Missouri is able to fight his own battles. The gallant west needs no aid
from the south to repel any attack which may be made on them from any
quarter. Let the gentleman from Massachusetts controvert the facts and
arguments of the gentleman from Missouri, if he can — and if he win the
victory, let him wear the honors; I shall not deprive him of his laurels.

The gentleman from Massachusetts, in reply to my remarks on the injurious operations of our land system on the prosperity of the west, pronounced an extravagant eulogium on the paternal care which the government had extended towards the west, to which he attributed all that was
great and excellent in the present condition of the new states. The language of the gentleman on this topic fell upon my ears like the almost
forgotten tones of the tory leaders of the British Parliament, at the commencement of the American revolution. They, too, discovered that the
colonies had grown great under the fostering care of the mother country; and I must confess, while listening to the gentleman, I thought the
appropriate reply to his argument was to be found in the remark of a
celebrated orator, made on that occasion : " They have grown great in
spite of your protection."

The gentleman, in commenting on the policy of the government in relation to the new states, has introduced to our notice a certain *Nathan
Dane*, of Massachusetts, to whom he attributes the celebrated ordinance of
'87, by which he tells us, "*slavery* was forever excluded from the new
states north of the Ohio." After eulogizing the wisdom of this provision
in terms of the most extravagant praise, he breaks forth in admiration of
the greatness of Nathan Dane — and great indeed he must be, if it be true,
as stated by the senator from Massachusetts, that " he was greater than
Solon and Lycurgus, Minos, Numa Pompilius, and all the legislators and
philosophers of the world," ancient and modern. Sir, to such high authority it is certainly my duty, in a becoming spirit of humility, to submit.
And yet, the gentleman will pardon me, when I say, that it is a little
unfortunate for the fame of this great legislator, that the gentleman from
Missouri should have proved that he was not the author of the ordinance
of '87, on which the senator from Massachusetts has reared so glorious a
monument to his name. Sir, I doubt not the senator will feel some com-
passion for our ignorance, when I tell him, that so little are we acquainted with the modern great men of New England, that until he informed
us yesterday that we possessed a Solon and a Lycurgus in the person of
Nathan Dane, he was only known to the south as a member of a celebrated assembly, called and known by the name of the " Hartford Convention." In the proceedings of that assembly, which I hold in my hand,
(at p. 19,) will be found, in a few lines, the history of Nathan Dane ;
and a little farther on, there is conclusive evidence of that ardent devotion to the interest of the new states, which, it seems, has given him a just
claim to the title of " Father of the West." By the 2d resolution of the
" Hartford Convention," it is declared, "that it is expedient to attempt

to make provision *for restraining Congress in the exercise of an unlimited power to make new states,* and admitting them into the Union." So much for Nathan Dane, of Beverly, Massachusetts.

In commenting upon my views in relation to the public lands, the gentleman insists, that it being one of the conditions of the grants that these lands should be applied to "the common benefit of all the states, they must always remain *a fund for revenue;*" and adds, "they must be *treated as so much treasure.*" Sir, the gentleman could hardly find language strong enough to convey his disapprobation of the policy which I had ventured to recommend to the favorable consideration of the country. And what, sir, was that policy, and what is the difference between that gentleman and myself on that subject? I threw out the idea that the public lands ought not to be reserved forever, as "a great fund for revenue;" that they ought not to be "treated as a great treasure;" but that the course of our policy should rather be directed towards the creation of new states, and building up great and flourishing communities.

Now, sir, will it be believed, by those who now hear me, — and who listened to the gentleman's denunciation of my doctrines yesterday, — that a book then lay open before him — nay, that he held it in his hand, and read from it certain passages of his own speech, delivered to the House of Representatives in 1825, in which speech he himself contended for the very doctrines I had advocated, and almost in the same terms? Here is the speech of the Hon. Daniel Webster, contained in the first volume of Gales and Seaton's Register of Debates, (p. 251,) delivered in the House of Representatives on the 18th of January, 1825, in a debate on the *Cumberland road* — the very debate from which the senator read yesterday. I shall read from the celebrated speech two passages, from which it will appear that both as to *the past* and the *future policy* of the government in relation to the public lands, the gentleman from Massachusetts maintained, in 1825, substantially the same opinions which I have advanced, but which he now so strongly reprobates. I said, sir, that the system of *credit sales* by which the west had been kept constantly in debt to the United States, and by which their wealth was drained off to be expended elsewhere, had operated injuriously on their prosperity. On this point the gentleman from Massachusetts, in January, 1825, expressed himself thus: "There could be no doubt, if gentlemen looked at the money received into the treasury from the sale of the public lands to the west, and then looked to the whole amount expended by government, (even including the whole amount of what was laid out for the army,) the latter must be allowed to be very inconsiderable, and *there must be a constant drain of money from the west to pay for the public lands.* It might indeed be said that this was no more than the refluence of capital which had previously gone over the mountains. Be it so. Still its practical effect was to produce inconvenience, *if not distress, by absorbing the money of the people.*"

I contended that the public lands ought not to be treated merely as "a fund for revenue;" that they ought not to be hoarded "as a great treasure." On this point the senator expressed himself thus: "Government, he believed, had received eighteen or twenty millions of dollars from the public lands, and it was with the greatest satisfaction he adverted to the change which had been introduced in the mode of paying for them; *yet he could never think the national domain was to be regarded as any great source of revenue.* The great object of the government, in respect of these lands, was not so much *the money derived from their sale,* as it was *the getting them settled.* What he meant to say was, *he did not think they ought to hug that domain* AS A GREAT TREASURE, *which was to enrich the Exchequer.*"

Now, Mr. President, it will be seen that the very doctrines which the gentleman so indignantly abandons were urged by him in 1825; and if I had actually borrowed my sentiments from those which he then avowed, I could not have followed more closely in his footsteps. Sir, it is only since the gentleman quoted this book, yesterday, that my attention has been turned to the sentiments he expressed in 1825; and if I had remembered them, I might possibly have been deterred from uttering sentiments here, which, it might well be supposed, I had borrowed from that gentleman.

In 1825, the gentleman told the world that the public lands " ought not to be treated as a treasure." He now tells us that "they must be treated as so much treasure." What the deliberate opinion of the gentleman on this subject may be, belongs not to me to determine; but I do not think he can, with the shadow of justice or propriety, impugn my sentiments, while his own recorded opinions are identical with my own. When the gentleman refers to the conditions of the grants under which the United States have acquired these lands, and insists that, as they are declared to be " for the common benefit of all the states," they can only be treated as so much treasure, I think he has applied a rule of construction too narrow for the case. If in the deeds of cession it has been declared that the grants were intended for " the common benefit of all the states," it is clear, from other provisions, that they were not intended merely as *so much property ;* for it is expressly declared, that the object of the grants is the erection of new states; and the United States, in accepting this trust, bind themselves to facilitate the foundation of these states, to be admitted into the Union with all the rights and privileges of the original states. This, sir, was the great end to which all parties looked, and it is by the fulfilment of this high trust that " the common benefit of all the states " is to be best promoted. Sir, let me tell the gentleman, that in the part of the country in which I live, we do not measure political benefits by the *money standard.* We consider as more valuable than gold liberty, principle, and justice. But, sir, if we are bound to act on the narrow principles contended for by the gentleman, I am wholly at a loss to conceive how he can reconcile his principles with his own practice. The lands are, it seems, to be treated " as so much treasure," and must be applied to the " common benefit of all the states." Now, if this be so, whence does he derive the right to appropriate them for partial and local objects? How can the gentleman consent to vote away immense bodies of these lands, for canals in Indiana and Illinois, to the Louisville and Portland Canal, to Kenyon College in Ohio, to Schools for the Deaf and Dumb, and other objects of a similar description? If grants of this character can fairly be considered as made " for the common benefit of all the states," it can only be, because all the states are interested in the welfare of each — a principle which, carried to the full extent, destroys all distinction between local and national objects, and is certainly *broad enough* to embrace the principles for which I have ventured to contend. Sir, the true difference between us I take to be this: the gentleman wishes to treat the public lands as a great treasure, just as so much money in the treasury, to be applied to all objects, constitutional and unconstitutional, to which the public money is constantly applied. I consider it as a sacred trust which we ought to fulfil, on the principles for which I have contended.

The senator from Massachusetts has thought proper to present, in strong contrast, the friendly feelings of the east towards the west, with sentiments of an opposite character displayed by the south in relation to appropriations for *internal improvements.* Now, sir, let it be recollected that the south have made no professions ; I have certainly made none in their behalf, of regard for the west. It has been reserved for the gentleman from Massachusetts, while he vaunts over his own personal devotion to western interests, to claim for the entire section of country to which he belongs an ardent friendship for the west, as manifested by their support of the system of internal improvement, while he casts in our teeth the reproach that the south has manifested hostility to western interests in opposing appropriations for such objects. That gentleman, at the same time, acknowledged that the south entertains *constitutional scruples* on this subject. Are we then, sir, to understand that the gentleman considers it a just subject of reproach that we respect our oaths, by which we are bound " to preserve, protect, and defend the constitution of the U. States ? " Would the gentleman have us manifest our love to the west by trampling under foot our constitutional scruples ? Does he not perceive, if the south is to *be reproached* with unkindness to the west, in voting against appropriations which the gentleman admits they could not vote for without doing violence to their constitutional opinions, that he exposes himself to the question, whether, if he was in our situation, he could vote for these appropriations, regardless of his scruples ? No, sir, I will not do the gentleman so great injustice. He has fallen into this error from not having duly weighed the force and effect of the reproach which he was endeavoring to cast upon the south. In relation to the other point, the friendship manifested by New England towards the west, in their support of the system of internal improvement, the gentleman will pardon me for saying, that I think he is equally unfortunate in having introduced that topic. As that gentleman has forced it upon us, however, I cannot suffer it to pass unnoticed. When the gentleman tells us that the appropriations for internal improvement in the west would, in almost every instance, have failed but for New England votes, he has forgotten to tell us the *when,* the *how,* and the *wherefore* this new-born zeal for the west sprung up in the bosom of New England. If we look back only a few years, we will find in both houses of Congress a uniform and steady opposition on the part of the members from the Eastern States, generally, to all appropriations of this character. At the time I became a member of this house, and for some time afterwards, a decided majority of the New England senators were opposed to the very measures which the senator from Massachusetts tells us they now cordially support. Sir, the Journals are before me, and an examination of them will satisfy every gentleman of that fact.

It must be well known to every one whose experience dates back as far as 1825, that up to a certain period, New England was generally opposed to appropriations for internal improvements in the west. The gentleman from Massachusetts may be himself an exception, but if he went for the system before 1825, it is certain that his colleagues did not go with him.

In the session of 1824 and '25, however, (a memorable era in the history of this country,) a wonderful change took place in New England, in relation to western interests. Sir, an extraordinary union of sympathies and of interests was then effected, which brought the east and the west into close alliance. The book from which I have before read contains the first public annunciation of that happy reconciliation of conflicting interests, personal and political, which brought the east and west together, and locked in a fraternal embrace the two great orators of the east and the west. Sir, it was on the 18th January, 1825, while the result of the presidential election, in the House of Representatives, was still doubtful, while the whole country was looking with intense anxiety to that legislative hall where the mighty drama was so soon to be acted, that we saw the leaders of two great parties in the house and in the nation, "taking sweet counsel together," and in a celebrated debate on the *Cumberland road*, fighting side by side for *western interests*. It was on that memorable occasion ,that the senator from Massachusetts *held out the white flag to the west*, and uttered those liberal sentiments which he yesterday so indignantly repudiated. Then it was, that that happy union between the members of the celebrated *coalition* was consummated, whose immediate issue was a president from *one quarter of the Union*, with the succession (as it was supposed) *secured to another.* The "American system," before a rude, disjointed, and misshapen mass, now assumed form and consistency. Then it was that it became "the settled policy of the government," that this system should be so administered as to create a reciprocity of interests and a reciprocal distribution of government favors, east and west, (the tariff and internal improvements,) while the south — yes, sir, the impracticable south — was to be "out of your protection." The gentleman may boast as much as he pleases of the friendship of New England for the west, as displayed in their support of internal improvement; but when he next introduces that topic, I trust that he will tell us *when* that friendship commenced, *how* it was brought about, and *why* it was established. Before I leave this topic, I must be permitted to say that the true character of the policy now pursued by the gentleman from Massachusetts and his friends, in relation to appropriations of land and money, for the benefit of the west, is in my estimation very similar to that pursued by Jacob of old towards his brother Esau : "it robs them of their birthright for a mess of pottage."

The gentleman from Massachusetts, in alluding to a remark of mine, that before any disposition could be made of the public lands, the *national debt* (for which they stand pledged) must be first paid, took occasion to intimate "that the *extraordinary fervor* which seems to exist in a *certain quarter*, (meaning the south, sir,) for the payment of the debt, arises from a disposition *to weaken the ties which bind the people to the Union.*" While the gentleman deals us this blow, he professes an ardent desire to see the debt speedily extinguished. He must excuse me, however, for feeling some distrust on that subject until I find this disposition manifested by something stronger than professions. I shall look for acts, decided and unequivocal acts ; for the performance of which will very soon (if I am not greatly mistaken) be afforded. Sir, if I were at liberty to judge of the course which that gentleman would pursue, from the principles which he has laid down in relation to this matter, I should be bound to conclude that he will be found acting with those with whom it is a darling object to prevent the payment of the public debt. He tells us he is desirous of paying the debt, "because we are under *an obligation* to discharge it." Now, sir, suppose it should happen that the public creditors, with whom we have contracted the obligation, should release us from it, so far as to declare their willingness to wait for payment for fifty years to come, provided only the interest shall be punctually discharged. The gentleman from Massachusetts will then be released from the obligation which now makes him desirous of paying the debt ; and, let me tell the gentleman, the holders of the stock will not only release us from this obligation, but they will implore, nay, they will even *pay us* not to pay them. But, adds the gentleman, so far as the debt may have an effect in binding the debtors to the country, and thereby serving as a link to hold the states together, he would be glad that it should exist forever. Surely then, sir, on the gentleman's own principles, he must be opposed to the payment of the debt.

Sir, let me tell that gentleman, that the south repudiates the idea that a *pecuniary dependence* on the federal government is one of the legitimate means of holding the states together. A moneyed interest in the government is essentially a base interest ; and just so far as it operates to bind the feelings of those who are subjected to it to the government, — just so far as it operates in creating sympathies and interests that would not otherwise exist, — is it opposed to all the principles of free government, and at war with virtue and patriotism. Sir, the link which binds the public creditors, *as such*, to their country, binds them equally to all governments, whether arbitrary or free. In a free government, this principle of abject dependence, if extended through all the ramifications of society, must be fatal to liberty. Already have we made alarming strides in that direction. The entire class of manufacturers, the holders of stocks, with their hundreds of millions of capital, are held to the government by the strong link of *pecuniary interests ;* millions of people — entire sections of country, interested, or believing themselves to be so, in the public lands, and the public treasure — are bound to the government by the expectation of *pecuniary favors*. If this system is carried much further, no man can fail to see that every generous motive of attachment to the country will be destroyed, and in its place will spring up those low, grovelling, base, and selfish feelings which bind men to the footstool of a despot by bonds as strong and enduring as those which attach them to free institutions. Sir, I would lay the foundation of this government in the affections of the people — I would teach them to cling to it by dispensing equal justice, and above all, by securing the "blessings of liberty " to "themselves and to their posterity."

The honorable gentleman from Massachusetts has gone out of his way to pass a high eulogium on the state of OHIO. In the most impassioned tones of eloquence, he described her majestic march to greatness. He told us, that, having already left all the other states far behind, she was now passing by Virginia and Pennsylvania, and about to take her station by the side of New York. To all this, sir, I was disposed most cordially to respond. When, however, the gentleman proceeded to contrast the state of Ohio with Kentucky, to the disadvantage of the latter, I listened to him with regret ; and when he proceeded further to attribute the great, and, as he supposed, acknowledged superiority of the former in population, wealth, and general prosperity, to the policy of Nathan Dane, of Massachusetts, which had secured to the people of Ohio (by the ordinance of '87) *a population of freemen*, I will confess that my feelings suffered a revulsion which I am now unable to describe in any language sufficiently respectful towards the gentleman from Massachusetts. In contrasting the state of Ohio with Kentucky, for the purpose of pointing out *the superiority of the former*, and of attributing that superiority to *the existence of slavery* in the one state, and its absence in the other, I

thought I could discern *the very spirit of the Missouri question,* intruded
into this debate, for objects best known to the gentleman himself. Did
that gentleman, sir, when he formed the determination to cross the
southern border, in order to invade the state of South Carolina, deem it
prudent or necessary to enlist under his banners *the prejudices of the
world,* which, like *Swiss troops,* may be engaged in any cause, and are
prepared to serve under any leader? Did he desire to avail himself of
those remorseless allies, *the passions of mankind,* of which it may be
more truly said than of the savage tribes of the wilderness, "that their
known rule of warfare is an indiscriminate slaughter of all ages, sexes,
and conditions"? Or was it supposed, sir, that, in a premeditated and
unprovoked attack upon the south, it was advisable to begin by a gentle
admonition of *our supposed weakness,* in order to prevent us from making
that firm and manly resistance due to our own character and our dearest
interests? Was the *significant hint* of the *weakness of slaveholding
states,* when contrasted with *the superior strength of free states,* — like the
glare of the weapon half drawn from its scabbard, — intended to enforce the
lessons of prudence and of patriotism, which the gentleman had resolved,
out of his abundant generosity, gratuitously to bestow upon us? Mr.
President, the impression which has gone abroad of the *weakness of the
south,* as connected with the *slave question,* exposes us to such constant
attacks, has done us so much injury, and is calculated to produce such
infinite mischiefs, that I embrace the occasion presented by the remarks
of the gentleman of Massachusetts, to declare that we are ready to meet
the question promptly and fearlessly. It is one from which we are not
disposed to shrink, in whatever form or under whatever circumstances it
may be pressed upon us.

We are ready to make up the issue with the gentleman, as to the influence of slavery on individual or national character — on the prosperity
and greatness, either of the United States or of particular states. Sir,
when arraigned before the bar of public opinion, on this charge of slavery,
we can stand up with conscious rectitude, plead not guilty, and put ourselves upon God and our country. Sir, we will not consent to look at
slavery in the abstract. We will not stop to inquire whether the black
man, as some philosophers have contended, is of an inferior race, nor
whether his color and condition are the effects of a curse inflicted for the
offences of his ancestors. We deal in no *abstractions.* We will not
look back to inquire whether our fathers were guiltless in introducing
slaves into this country. If an inquiry should ever be instituted in these
matters, however, it will be found that the profits of the slave trade were
not confined to the south. Southern ships and southern sailors were not
the instruments of bringing slaves to the shores of America, nor did our
merchants reap the profits of that "accursed traffic." But, sir, we will
pass over all this. If slavery, as it now exists in this country, be an
evil, we of the present day *found it ready made to our hands.* Finding
our lot cast among a people whom God had manifestly committed to our
care, we did not sit down to speculate on abstract questions of theoretical
liberty. We met it as a practical question of *obligation and duty.* We
resolved to make the best of the situation in which Providence had placed
us, and to fulfil the high trusts which had devolved upon us as the owners
of slaves, in the only way in which such a trust could be fulfilled, without
spreading misery and ruin throughout the land. We found that we had
to deal with a people whose physical, moral, and intellectual habits and

character totally disqualified them from the enjoyment of the blessings of freedom. We could not send them back to the shores from whence their fathers had been taken; their numbers forbade the thought, even if we did not know that their condition here is infinitely preferable to what it possibly could be among the barren sands and savage tribes of Africa; and it was wholly irreconcilable with all our notions of humanity to tear asunder the tender ties which they had formed among us, to gratify the feelings of a false philanthropy. What a commentary on the wisdom, justice, and humanity of the southern slave owner is presented by the example of certain benevolent associations and charitable individuals *elsewhere!* Shedding weak tears over sufferings which had existence in their own sickly imaginations, these "friends of humanity" set themselves systematically to work to seduce the slaves of the south from their masters. By means of missionaries and political tracts, the scheme was in a great measure successful. Thousands of these deluded victims of fanaticism were seduced into the enjoyment of freedom in our northern cities. And what has been the consequence? Go to these cities now and ask the question. Visit the dark and narrow lanes, and obscure recesses, which have been assigned by common consent as the abodes of those outcasts of the world, the free people of color. Sir, there does not exist, on the face of the whole earth, a population so poor, so wretched, so vile, so loathsome, so utterly destitute of all the comforts, conveniences, and decencies of life, as the unfortunate blacks of Philadelphia, and New York, and Boston. Liberty has been to them the greatest of calamities, the heaviest of curses. Sir, I have had some opportunities of making comparison between the condition of the free negroes of the north and the slaves of the south, and the comparison has left not only an indelible impression of the superior advantages of the latter, but has gone far to reconcile me to slavery itself. Never have I felt so forcibly that touching description, "the foxes have holes, and the birds of the air have nests, but the Son of man hath not where to lay his head," as when I have seen this unhappy race, naked and houseless, almost starving in the streets, and abandoned by all the world. Sir, I have seen in the neighborhood of one of the most moral, religious, and refined cities of the north, a family of free blacks, driven to the caves of the rocks, and there obtaining a precarious subsistence from charity and plunder.

When the gentleman from Massachusetts adopts and reiterates the old charge of weakness as resulting from slavery, I must be permitted to call for the proof of those blighting effects which he ascribes to its influence. I suspect that when the subject is closely examined, it will be found that there is not much force even in the plausible objection of the want of physical power in slaveholding states. The power of a country is compounded of its population and its wealth, and in modern times, where, from the very form and structure of society, by far the greater portion of the people must, even during the continuance of the most desolating wars, be employed in the cultivation of the soil and other peaceful pursuits, it may be well doubted whether slaveholding states, by reason of the superior value of their productions, are not able to maintain a number of troops in the field fully equal to what could be supported by states with a larger white population, but not possessed of equal resources.

It is a popular error to suppose that, in any possible state of things, the people of a country could ever be called out *en masse*, or that a half, or a third, or even a fifth part of the physical force of any country could ever be brought into the field. The difficulty is, not to procure men, but to provide *the means of maintaining them;* and in this view of the subject, it may be asked whether the Southern States are not a source of *strength* and *power,* and not of *weakness,* to the country — whether they have not contributed, and are not now contributing, largely to the wealth and prosperity of every state in this Union. From a statement which I hold in my hand, it appears that in ten years — from 1818 to 1827, inclusive — the whole amount of the domestic exports of the United States was $521,811,045 ; of which three articles, *(the product of slave labor,)* viz., cotton, rice, and tobacco, amounted to $339,203,232 — equal to *about two thirds of the whole.* It is not true, as has been supposed, that the advantage of this labor is confined almost exclusively to the Southern States. Sir, I am thoroughly convinced that, at this time, *the states north of the Potomac actually derive greater profits from the labor of our slaves than we do ourselves.* It appears from our public documents, that in seven years — from 1821 to 1827, inclusive — the six Southern States *exported* $190,337,281, and *imported* only $55,646,301. Now, the difference between these two sums (near $140,000,000) *passed through the hands of the northern merchants,* and enabled them to carry on their commercial operations with all the world. Such part of these goods as found its way back to our hands came charged with the duties, as well as the profits, of the merchant, the ship owner, and a host of others, who found employment in carrying on these immense exchanges ; and for such part as was consumed at the north, we received in exchange *northern manufactures,* charged with an increased price, to cover all the taxes which the northern consumer had been compelled to pay on the imported article. It will be seen, therefore, at a glance, how much slave labor has contributed to the wealth and prosperity of the United States, and how largely our northern brethren have participated in the profits of that labor. Sir, on this subject I will quote an authority, which will, I doubt not, be considered by the senator from Massachusetts as entitled to high respect. It is from the great father of the "American System," *honest Matthew Carey* — no great friend, it is true, at this time, to southern rights and southern interests, but not the worst authority on that account, *on the point in question.*

Speaking of the *relative importance to the Union* of the SOUTHERN and the EASTERN STATES, Matthew Carey, in the sixth edition of his Olive Branch, (p. 278,) after exhibiting a number of statistical tables to show the decided superiority of the former, thus proceeds : —

"But I am tired of this investigation — I sicken for the honor of the human species. What idea must the world form of the arrogance of the pretensions or the one side, [the east,] and of the folly and weakness of the rest of the Union, to have so long suffered them to pass without exposure and detection. The naked fact is, that the demagogues in the Eastern States, not satisfied *with deriving all the benefit from the southern section of the Union that they would from so many wealthy colonies* — with making princely fortunes by the carriage and exportation of its bulky and valuable productions, and *supplying it with their own manufactures,* and the productions of Europe and the East and West Indies, to an enormous amount, and at an immense profit, have uniformly treated it with outrage, insult, and injury. And, regardless of their vital interests, the Eastern States were lately *courting their own destruction,* by allowing a few restless turbulent men to lead them blindfolded *to a separation* which was *pregnant with their certain ruin.* Whenever that event takes place, they sink into insignificance. If a separation were desirable to any part of the Union, it would be to the Middle and Southern States, particularly the latter, who have been so long harassed with the complaints, the restlessness, the turbulence, and the ingratitude of the Eastern States, that their patience has been tried almost beyond endurance. '*Jeshurun waxed fat and kicked*' — and he will be severely punished for his kicking, in the event ᴏf a dissolution of the Union." Sir, I wish it to be distinctly understood that I do not adopt these sentiments as my own. I quote them to show that very different sentiments have prevailed in former times as to the weakness of the slaveholding states from those which now seem to have become fashionable in certain quarters. I know it has been supposed by certain ill-informed persons, that the south exists only by the countenance and protection of the north. Sir, this is the idlest of all idle and ridiculous fancies that ever entered into the mind of man. In every state of this Union, except one, the free white population actually preponderates ; while in the British West India Islands, (where the average white population is *less than ten per cent. of the whole,*) the slaves are kept in entire subjection : it is preposterous to suppose that the Southern States could ever find the smallest difficulty in this respect. On this subject, as in all others, we ask nothing of our northern brethren but to "let us alone." Leave us to the undisturbed management of our domestic concerns, and the direction of our own industry, and we will ask no more. Sir, all our difficulties on this subject have arisen from interference from abroad, which has disturbed, and may again disturb, our domestic tranquillity just so far as to bring down punishment upon the heads of the unfortunate victims of a fanatical and mistaken humanity.

There is *a spirit*, which, like the father of evil, is constantly "walking to and fro about the earth, seeking whom it may devour :" it is the spirit of FALSE PHILANTHROPY. The persons whom it possesses do not indeed throw themselves into the flames, but they are employed in lighting up the torches of discord throughout the community. Their first principle of action is to leave their own affairs, and neglect their own duties, to regulate the affairs and duties of others. Theirs is the task to feed the hungry, and clothe the naked, of other lands, while they thrust the naked, famished, and shivering beggar from their own doors ; to instruct the heathen, while their own children want the bread of life. When this spirit infuses itself into the bosom of a statesman, (if one so possessed can be called a statesman,) it converts him at once into a visionary enthusiast. Then it is that he indulges in golden dreams of national greatness and prosperity. He discovers that "liberty is power," and not content with vast schemes of improvement at home, which it would bankrupt the treasury of the world to execute, he flies to foreign lands, to fulfil obligations to "the human race" by inculcating the principles of "political and religious liberty," and promoting the "general welfare" of the whole human race. It is a spirit which has long been busy with the *slaves of the south ;* and is even now displaying itself in vain efforts to drive the government from its wise policy in relation to the *Indians.* It is this spirit which has filled the land with thousands of wild and visionary projects, which can have no effect but to waste the energies and dissipate the resources of the country. It is the spirit of which the aspiring politician dexterously avails himself, when, by inscribing on his banner the magical words LIBERTY and PHILANTHROPY, he draws to his support that class of persons who are ready to bow down at the very name of their idols.

But, sir, whatever difference of opinion may exist as to the effect of slavery on national wealth and prosperity, if we may trust to experience, there can be no doubt that it has never yet produced any injurious effect on *individual or national character.* Look through the whole history of the country, from the commencement of the revolution down to the present hour ; where are there to be found brighter examples of intellectual and moral greatness than have been exhibited by the sons of the south? From the FATHER OF HIS COUNTRY down to the DISTINGUISHED CHIEF-TAIN who has been elevated by a grateful people to the highest office in their gift, the interval is filled up by a long line of orators, of statesmen, and of heroes, justly entitled to rank among the ornaments of their country, and the benefactors of mankind. Look at the "Old Dominion," great and magnanimous Virginia, "whose jewels are her sons." Is there any state in this Union which has contributed so much to the honor and welfare of the country? Sir, I will yield the whole question—I will acknowledge the fatal effects of slavery upon character, if any one can say, that for noble disinterestedness, ardent love of country, exalted virtue, and a pure and holy devotion to liberty, the people of the Southern States have ever been surpassed by any in the world. I know, sir, that this *devotion to liberty* has sometimes been supposed to be at war with our institutions ; but it is in some degree the result of those very institutions. Burke, the most philosophical of statesmen, as he was the most accomplished of orators, well understood the operation of this principle, in elevating the sentiments and exalting the principles of the people in slaveholding states I will conclude my remarks on this branch of the subject, by reading a few passages from his speech "on moving his resolutions for conciliation with the colonies," the 22d of March, 1775.

"There is a circumstance attending the southern colonies which makes the spirit of liberty still more high and haughty than in those to the northward. It is, that in Virginia and the Carolinas they have a *vast multitude of slaves.* Where this is the case, in any part of the world, those who are free are by far the most proud and jealous of their freedom. Freedom is to them not only an enjoyment, but a kind of rank and privilege. Not seeing there, as in countries where it is a common blessing, and as broad and general as the air, that it may be united with much abject toil, with great misery, with all the exterior of servitude, liberty looks among them like something more noble and liberal. I do not mean, sir, to commend the superior morality of this sentiment, which has, at least, as much pride as virtue in it — but I cannot alter the nature of man. The fact is so ; and these people of the southern colonies are much more strongly, and with a higher and more stubborn spirit, attached to liberty than those to the northward. Such were all the ancient commonwealths — such were our Gothic ancestors — such, in our days, were the Poles — *and such will be all masters of slaves who are not slaves themselves.* In such a people, the haughtiness of domination combines with the spirit of freedom, fortifies it, *and renders it invincible.*"

In the course of my former remarks, Mr. President, I took occasion to deprecate, as one of the greatest evils, *the consolidation of this government.* The gentleman takes alarm at the sound. " Consolidation," "like the tar-*iff*," grates upon his ear. He tells us, " we have heard much of late about consolidation ; that it is the rallying word of all who are endeavoring to *weaken the Union*, by adding to the power of the states." But consolidation (says the gentleman) was the very object for which the Union was formed ; and, in support of that opinion, he read a passage from the address of the president of the convention to Congress, which he assumes to be authority on his side of the question. But, sir, the gentleman is mistaken. The object of the framers of the constitution, as disclosed in that address, was not the *consolidation of the government*, but " the consolidation of the Union." It was not to draw power from the states, in order to transfer it to a great national government, but, in the language of the constitution itself, " to form a more perfect Union ; " — and by what means ? By "establishing justice, promoting domestic tranquillity, and securing the blessings of liberty to ourselves and our posterity." This is the true reading of the constitution. But, according to the gentleman's reading, the object of the constitution was, to *consolidate the government*, and the means would seem to be, the promotion of *injustice*, causing domestic *discord*, and depriving the states and the people " of the blessings of liberty " forever.

The gentleman boasts of belonging to the party of NATIONAL REPUBLICANS. National Republicans! A new name, sir, for a very old thing. The National Republicans of the present day were the *Federalists* of '98, who became *Federal Republicans* during the war of 1812, and were *manufactured* into *National Republicans* somewhere about the year 1825.

As a party, (by whatever name distinguished,) they have always been animated by the same principles, and have kept steadily in view a common object, the consolidation of the government. Sir, the party to which I am proud of having belonged, from the very commencement of my political life to the present day, were the *Democrats of '98*, (*Anarchists, Anti-Federalists, Revolutionists*, I think they were sometimes called.) They assumed the name of *Democratic Republicans* in 1822, and have retained their name and principles up to the present hour. True to their political faith, they have always, as a party, been in favor of limitations of power ; they have insisted that all powers not delegated to the federal government are reserved, and have been constantly struggling, as they now are, to preserve the rights of the states, and to prevent them from being drawn into the vortex, and swallowed up by one great consolidated government.

Sir, any one acquainted with the history of parties in this country will recognize in the points now in dispute between the senator from Massachusetts and myself the very grounds which have, from the beginning, divided the two great parties in this country, and which (call these parties by what names you will, and *amalgamate* them as you may) will divide them forever. The true distinction between those parties is laid down in a celebrated manifesto, issued by the convention of the Federalists of Massachusetts, assembled in Boston, in February, 1824, on the occasion of organizing a party opposition to the reëlection of Governor Eustis. The gentleman will recognize this as " the canonical book of political scripture ; " and it instructs us that, when the American colonies redeemed themselves from British bondage, and became so many *independent nations*, they proposed to form a NATIONAL UNION, (not a *Federal* Union, sir, but a National Union.) Those who were in favor of a *union of the states in this form* became known by the name of *Federalists ;* those who wanted no union of the states, or disliked the proposed form of union, became known by the name of *Anti-Federalists.* By means which need not be enumerated, the *Anti-Federalists* became (after the expiration of twelve years) our national rulers, and for a period of sixteen years, until the close of Mr. Madison's administration, in 1817, continued to exercise the exclusive direction of our public affairs. Here, sir, is the true history of the origin, rise, and progress of the party of *National Republicans,* who date back to the very origin of the government, and who, then, as now, chose to consider the constitution as having created, not a *Federal,* but a *National Union ;* who regarded "consolidation" as no evil, and who doubtless consider it "a consummation devoutly to be wished" to build up a great "central government," "one and indivisible." Sir, there have existed, in every age and every country, two distinct orders of men — the *lovers of freedom,* and the devoted *advocates of power.*

The same great leading principles, modified only by the peculiarities of manners, habits, and institutions, divided parties in the ancient republics, animated the *whigs* and *tories* of Great Britain, distinguished in our own times the *liberals* and *ultras* of France, and may be traced even in the bloody struggles of unhappy Spain. Sir, when the gallant *Riego,* who devoted himself, and all that he possessed, to the liberties of his country, was dragged to the scaffold, followed by the tears and lamentations of every lover of freedom throughout the world, he perished amid the deafening cries of "Long live the absolute king!" The people whom I represent, Mr. President, are the descendants of those who brought with them to this country, as the most precious of their possessions, "an ardent love of liberty;" and while that shall be preserved, they will always be found manfully struggling against the *consolidation of the government* — AS THE WORST OF EVILS.

The senator from Massachusetts, in alluding to the tariff, becomes quite facetious. He tells us that "he hears of nothing but *tariff, tariff, tariff ;* and, if a word could be found to rhyme with it, he presumes it would be celebrated in verse, and set to music." Sir, perhaps the gentleman, *in mockery of our complaints,* may be himself disposed to sing the praises of the tariff, in doggerel verse, to the tune of "Old Hundred." I am not at all surprised, however, at the aversion of the gentleman to the very name of *tariff.* I doubt not that it must always bring up some very unpleasant recollections to his mind. If I am not greatly mistaken, the senator from Massachusetts was a leading actor at a great meeting got up in Boston, in 1820, *against the tariff.* It has generally been supposed that he drew up the resolutions adopted by that meeting, denouncing the tariff system as unequal, oppressive, and unjust, and if I am not much mistaken, *denying its constitutionality.* Certain it is, that the gentleman made a speech on that occasion in support of those resolutions, denouncing the system in no very measured terms ; and, if my memory serves me, *calling its constitutionality in question.* I regret that I have not been able to lay my hands on those proceedings ; but I have seen them, and cannot be mistaken in their character. At that time, sir, the senator from Massachusetts entertained the very sentiments in relation to the tariff which the south now entertains. We next find the senator from Massachusetts expressing his opinion on the tariff, as a member of the House of Representatives from the city of Boston, in 1824. On that occasion, sir, the gentleman assumed a position which commanded the respect and admiration of his country. He stood forth the powerful and fearless champion of *free trade.* He met, in that conflict, the advocates of restriction and monopoly, and they " fled from before his face." With a profound sagacity, a fulness of knowledge, and a richness of illustration that have never been surpassed, he maintained and established the principles of commercial freedom, on a foundation never to be shaken. Great indeed was the victory achieved by the gentleman on that occasion ; most striking the contrast between the clear, forcible, and convincing arguments by which he carried away the understandings of his hearers, and the narrow views and wretched sophistry of *another distinguished orator,* who may be truly said to have " held up his farthing candle to the sun."

Sir, the senator from Massachusetts, on that, the proudest day of his life, like a mighty giant, bore away upon his shoulders the pillars of the temple of error and delusion, escaping himself unhurt, and leaving his adversaries overwhelmed in its ruins. Then it was that he erected to free trade a beautiful and enduring monument, and "inscribed the marble with his name." Mr. President, it is with pain and regret that I now go forward to the next great era in the political life of that gentleman, when he was found on this floor, supporting, advocating, and finally voting for the tariff of 1828 — that "bill of abominations." By that act, sir, the senator from Massachusetts has destroyed the labors of his whole life, and given a wound to the cause of free trade never to be healed. , Sir, when I recollect the position which that gentleman once occupied, and that which he now holds in public estimation, in relation to this subject, it is not at all surprising that the tariff should be hateful to his ears. Sir, if I had erected to my own fame so proud a monument as that which the gentleman built up in 1824, and I could have been tempted to destroy it with my own hands, I should hate the voice that should ring "the accursed tariff" in my ears. I doubt not the gentleman feels very much, in relation to the tariff, as a certain knight did to "*instinct,*" and with him would be disposed to exclaim, —

"Ah ! no more of that, Hal, an thou lovest me."

But, Mr. President, to be more serious ; what are we of the south to think of what we have heard this day ? The senator from Massachusetts tells us that the tariff is not an eastern measure, and treats it as if the east had no interest in it. The senator from Missouri insists it is not a western measure, and that it has done no good to the west. The south comes in, and, in the most earnest manner, represents to you that this measure, which we are told " is of no value to the east or the west," is " utterly destructive of our interests." We represent to you that it has spread ruin and devastation through the land, and prostrated our hopes in the dust. We solemnly declare that we believe the system to be wholly unconstitutional, and a violation of the compact between the states and the Union ; and our brethren *turn a deaf ear to our complaints,* and refuse to relieve us from a system " which not enriches them, but makes us poor indeed." Good God ! Mr. President, *has it come to this?* Do gentlemen hold the feelings and wishes of their brethren at so cheap a rate, that they refuse to gratify them at so small a price ? Do gentlemen value so lightly the peace and harmony of the country, that they will not yield a measure of this description to the affectionate entreaties and earnest remonstrances of their friends ? Do gentlemen estimate the value of the Union at so low a price, that they will not even

make one effort to bind the states together with the cords of affection?
And has it come to this? Is this the spirit in which this government
is to be administered? If so, let me tell gentlemen, the seeds of dissolu
tion are already sown, and our children will reap the bitter fruit.

The honorable gentleman from Massachusetts, (Mr. Webster,) while
he exonerates me personally from the charge, intimates that there is a
party in the country who are looking to disunion. Sir, if the gentleman
had stopped there, the accusation would have " passed by me like the
idle wind, which I regard not." But when he goes on to give to his
accusation " a local habitation and a name," by quoting the expression of
a distinguished citizen of South Carolina, (Dr. Cooper,) " that it was time
for the south to calculate the value of the Union," and in the language
of the bitterest sarcasm, adds, " Surely then the Union cannot last longer
than July, 1831," it is impossible to mistake either the allusion or the
object of the gentleman. Now, Mr. President, I call upon every one
who hears me to bear witness that this controversy is not of my seeking.
The Senate will do me the justice to remember that, at the time this
unprovoked and uncalled-for attack was made on the south, not one word
had been uttered by me in disparagement of New England ; nor had I
made the most distant allusion either to the senator from Massachusetts
or the state he represents. But, sir, that gentleman has thought proper,
for purposes best known to himself, to strike the south, through me, the
most unworthy of her servants. He has crossed the border, he has invaded the state of South Carolina, is making war upon her citizens, and
endeavoring to overthrow her principles and her institutions. Sir, when
the gentleman provokes me to such a conflict, I meet him at the thresh-
old ; I will struggle, while I have life, for our altars and our firesides ,
and, if God gives me strength, I will drive back the invader discomfited.
Nor shall I stop there. If the gentleman provokes the war, he shall
have war. Sir, I will not stop at the border ; I will carry the war into
the enemy's territory, and not consent to lay down my arms until I have
obtained " indemnity for the past and security for the future." It is
with unfeigned reluctance, Mr. President, that I enter upon the performance of this part of my duty ; I shrink almost instinctively from a course,
however necessary, which may have a tendency to excite sectional feelings and sectional jealousies. But, sir, the task has been forced upon
me ; and I proceed right onward to the performance of my duty. Be the
consequences what they may, the responsibility is with those who have
imposed upon me this necessity. The senator from Massachusetts has
thought proper to cast the first stone ; and if he shall find, according to a
homely adage, "that he lives in a glass house," on his head be the consequences. The gentleman has made a great flourish about his fidelity
to Massachusetts. I shall make no professions of zeal for the interests
and honor of South Carolina ; of that my constituents shall judge. If
there be one state in the Union, Mr. President, (and I say it not in a
boastful spirit,) that may challenge comparison with any other, for a
uniform, zealous, ardent, and uncalculating devotion to the Union, that
state is South Carolina. Sir, from the very commencement of the revolution up to this hour, there is no sacrifice, however great, she has not
cheerfully made, no service she has ever hesitated to perform. She has
adhered to you in your prosperity ; but in your adversity she has clung
to you with more than filial affection. No matter what was the condition
of her domestic affairs, though deprived of her resources, divided by

parties, or surrounded with difficulties, the call of the country has been to her as the voice of God. Domestic discord ceased at the sound; every man became at once reconciled to his brethren, and the sons of Carolina were all seen crowding together to the temple, bringing their gifts to the altar of their common country.

What, sir, was the conduct of the south during the revolution? Sir, I honor New England for her conduct in that glorious struggle. But great as is the praise which belongs to her, I think, at least, equal honor is due to the south. They espoused the quarrel of their brethren with a generous zeal, which did not suffer them to stop to calculate their interest in the dispute. Favorites of the mother country, possessed of neither ships nor seamen to create a commercial rivalship, they might have found in their situation a guaranty that their trade would be forever fostered and protected by Great Britain. But, trampling on all considerations either of interest or of safety, they rushed into the conflict, and fighting for principle, perilled all, in the sacred cause of freedom. Never was there exhibited in the history of the world higher examples of noble daring, dreadful suffering, and heroic endurance, than by the whigs of Carolina during the revolution. The whole state, from the mountains to the sea, was overrun by an overwhelming force of the enemy. The fruits of industry perished on the spot where they were produced, or were consumed by the foe. The "plains of Carolina" drank up the most precious blood of her citizens. Black and smoking ruins marked the places which had been the habitations of her children. Driven from their homes into the gloomy and almost impenetrable swamps, even there the spirit of liberty survived, and South Carolina (sustained by the example of her Sumpters and her Marions) proved, by her conduct, that though her soil might be overrun, the spirit of her people was invincible.

But, sir, our country was soon called upon to engage in another revolutionary struggle, and that, too, was a struggle for principle. I mean the political revolution which dates back to '98, and which, if it had not been successfully achieved, would have left us none of the fruits of the revolution of '76. The revolution of '98 restored the constitution, rescued the liberty of the citizen from the grasp of those who were aiming at its life, and in the emphatic language of Mr. Jefferson, "saved the constitution at its last gasp." And by whom was it achieved? By the south, sir, aided only by the democracy of the north and west.

I come now to the war of 1812 — a war which, I well remember, was called in derision (while its event was doubtful) the southern war, and sometimes the Carolina war; but which is now universally acknowledged to have done more for the honor and prosperity of the country than all other events in our history put together. What, sir, were the objects of that war? "Free trade and sailors' rights!" It was for the protection of northern shipping and New England seamen that the country flew to arms. What interest had the south in that contest? If they had sat down coldly to calculate the value of their interests involved in it, they would have found that they had every thing to lose, and nothing to gain. But, sir, with that generous devotion to country so characteristic of the south, they only asked if the rights of any portion of their fellow-citizens had been invaded; and when told that northern ships and New England seamen had been arrested on the common highway of nations, they felt that the honor of their country was assailed; and acting on that exalted sentiment "which feels a stain like a wound," they resolved to seek, in open war, for a redress of those injuries which it did not become freemen to endure. Sir, the whole south, animated as by a common impulse, cordially united in declaring and promoting that war. South Carolina sent to your councils, as the advocates and supporters of that war, the noblest of her sons. How they fulfilled that trust let a grateful country tell. Not a measure was adopted, not a battle fought, not a victory won, which contributed, in any degree, to the success of that war, to which southern councils and southern valor did not largely contribute. Sir, since South Carolina is assailed, I must be suffered to speak it to her praise, that at the very moment when, in one quarter, we heard it solemnly proclaimed, "that it did not become a religious and moral people to rejoice at the victories of our army or our navy, " her legislature unanimously

"*Resolved,* That we will cordially support the government in the vigorous prosecution of the war, until a peace can be obtained on honorable terms, and we will cheerfully submit to every privation that may be required of us, by our government, for the accomplishment of this object."

South Carolina redeemed that pledge. She threw open her treasury to the government. She put at the absolute disposal of the officers of the United States all that she possessed — her men, her money, and her arms. She appropriated half a million of dollars, on her own account, in defence of her maritime frontier, ordered a brigade of state troops to be raised, and when left to protect herself by her own means, never suffered the enemy to touch her soil, without being instantly driven off or captured.

Such, sir, was the conduct of the south — such the conduct of my own state in that dark hour "which tried men's souls."

When I look back and contemplate the spectacle exhibited at that time in another quarter of the Union — when I think of the conduct of certain portions of New England, and remember the part which was acted on that memorable occasion by the political associates of the gentleman from Massachusetts — nay, when I follow that gentleman into the councils of the nation, and listen to his voice during the darkest period of the war, I am indeed astonished that he should venture to touch upon the topics which he has introduced into this debate. South Carolina reproached by Massachusetts! And from whom does the accusation come? Not from the democracy of New England; for they have been in times past, as they are now, the friends and allies of the south. No, sir, the accusation comes from that party whose acts, during the most trying and eventful period of our national history, were of such a character, that their own legislature, but a few years ago, actually blotted them out from their records, as a stain upon the honor of the country. But how can they ever be blotted out from the recollection of any one who had a heart to feel, a mind to comprehend, and a memory to retain, the events of that day! Sir, I shall not attempt to write the history of the party in New England to which I have alluded — the war party in peace, and the peace party in war. That task I shall leave to some future biographer of Nathan Dane, and I doubt not it will be found quite easy to prove that the peace party of Massachusetts were the only defenders of their country during their war, and actually achieved all our victories by land and sea. In the mean time, sir, and until that history shall be written, I propose, with the feeble and glimmering lights which I possess, to review the conduct of this party, in connection with the war, and the events which immediately preceded it.

It will be recollected, sir, that our great causes of quarrel with Great Britain were her depredations on northern commerce, and the impresment of New England seamen.   From every quarter we were called upon for protection.   Importunate as the west is now represented to be on another subject, the importunity of the east on that occasion was far greater.   I hold in my hands the evidence of the fact.   Here are petitions, memorials, and remonstrances from all parts of New England, setting forth the injustice, the oppressions, the depredations, the insults, the outrages committed by Great Britain against the unoffending commerce and seamen of New England, and calling upon Congress for redress. Sir, I cannot stop to read these memorials.   In that from Boston, after stating the alarming and extensive condemnation of our vessels by Great Britain, which threatened " to sweep our commerce from the face of the ocean," and " to involve our merchants in bankruptcy," they call upon the government " to assert our rights, and to adopt such measures as will support the dignity and honor of the United States."

From Salem we heard a language still more decisive ; they call explicitly for " an appeal to arms," and pledge their lives and property in support of any measures which Congress might adopt.   From Newburyport an appeal was made " to the firmness and justice of the government to obtain compensation and protection."   It was here, I think, that, when the war was declared, it was resolved " to resist our own government even unto blood."   (Olive Branch, p. 101.)

In other quarters the common language of that day was, that our commerce and our seamen were entitled to protection ; and that it was the duty of the government to afford it at every hazard.   The conduct of Great Britain, we were then told, was " an outrage upon our national independence."   These clamors, which commenced as early as January, 1806, were continued up to 1812.   In a message from the governor of one of the New England States, as late as the 10th October, 1811, this language is held : " A manly and decisive course has become indispensable ; a course to satisfy foreign nations, that, while we desire peace, we have the means and the spirit to repel aggression.   We are false to ourselves when our commerce, or our territory, is invaded with impunity."

About this time, however, a remarkable change was observable in the tone and temper of those who had been endeavoring to force the country into a war.   The language of complaint was changed into that of insult, and calls for protection converted into reproaches.   " Smoke, smoke ! " says one writer ; " my life on it, our executive have no more idea of declaring war than my grandmother."   The committee of ways and means," says another, " have come out with their Pandora's box of taxes, and yet nobody dreams of war."   " Congress do not mean to declare war ; they dare not."   But why multiply examples ?   An honorable member of the other house, from the city of Boston, [Mr. Quincy,] in a speech delivered on the 3d April, 1812, says, " Neither promises, nor threats, nor asseverations, nor oaths, will make me believe that you will go to war.   The navigation states are sacrificed, and the spirit and character of the country prostrated by fear and avarice."   " You cannot, said the same gentleman, on another occasion, " be kicked into a war."

Well, sir, the war at length came, and what did we behold ?   The very men who had been for six years clamorous for war, and for whose protection it was waged, became at once equally clamorous against it.   They had received a miraculous visitation ; a new light suddenly beamed upon their minds ; the scales fell from their eyes, and it was discovered that the war was declared from " subserviency to France ; " and that Congress,

and the executive, "had sold themselves to Napoleon; ' that Great Britain had in fact " done us no essential injury ; " that she was " the bulwark
of our religion;" that where " she took one of our ships, she protected
twenty ; " and that, if Great Britain had impressed a few of our seamen,
it was because " she could not distinguish them from their own." And so
far did this spirit extend, that a committee of the Massachusetts legislature actually fell to calculation, and discovered, to their infinite satisfaction, but to the astonishment of all the world besides, that only eleven
Massachusetts sailors had ever been impressed.   Never shall I forget
the appeals that had been made to the sympathies of the south in behalf
of the " thousands of impressed Americans," who had been torn from their
families and friends, and " immured in the floating dungeons of Britain."
The most touching pictures were drawn of the hard condition of the American sailor, " treated like a slave," forced to fight the battles of his enemy,
" lashed to the mast, to be shot at like a dog."   But, sir, the very moment
we had taken up arms in their defence, it was discovered that all these
were mere " fictions of the brain ; " and that the whole number in the state
of Massachusetts was but eleven ; and that even these had been " taken
by mistake."   Wonderful discovery ! The secretary of state had collected
authentic lists of no less than six thousand impressed Americans.   Lord
Castlereagh himself acknowledged sixteen hundred.   Calculations on the
basis of the number found on board of the Guerriere, the Macedonian,
the Java, and other British ships, (captured by the skill and gallantry of
those heroes whose achievements are the treasured monuments of their
country's glory,) fixed the number at seven thousand ; and yet, it seems,
Massachusetts had lost but eleven ! Eleven Massachusetts sailors taken
by mistake ! A cause of war indeed ! Their ships too, the capture of
which had threatened " universal bankruptcy," it was discovered that
Great Britain was their friend and protector ; " where she had taken one
she had protected twenty." Then was the discovery made, that subserviency to France, hostility to commerce, " a determination, on the part
of the south and west, to break down the Eastern States," and especially
as reported by a committee of the Massachusetts legislature) " to force
the sons of commerce to populate the wilderness," were the true causes
of the war."   (Olive Branch, pp. 134, 291.) But let us look a little further into the conduct of the peace party of New England at that important crisis. Whatever difference of opinion might have existed as to
the causes of the war, the country had a right to expect, that, when once
involved in the contest, all America would have cordially united in its
support. Sir, the war effected, in its progress, a union of all parties at
the south. But not so in New England ; there great efforts were made
to stir up the minds of the people to oppose it. Nothing was left undone
to embarrass the financial operations of the government, to prevent the
enlistment of troops, to keep back the men and money of New England
from the service of the Union, to force the president from his seat. Yes,
sir, " the Island of Elba, or a halter ! " were the alternatives they presented to the excellent and venerable James Madison. Sir, the war was
further opposed by openly carrying on illicit trade with the enemy, by
permitting that enemy to establish herself on the very soil of Massachusetts, and by opening a free trade between Great Britain and America,
with a separate custom house. Yes, sir, those who cannot endure the
thought that we should insist on a free trade, in time of profound peace,
could, without scruple, claim and exercise the right of carrying on a free

trade with the enemy in a time of war; and finally by getting up the renowned "Hartford Convention," and preparing the way for an open resistance to the government, and a separation of the states. Sir, if I am asked for the proof of those things, I fearlessly appeal to contemporary history, to the public documents of the country, to the recorded opinion and acts of public assemblies, to the declaration and acknowledgments, since made, of the executive and legislature of Massachusetts herself.*

Sir, the time has not been allowed me to trace this subject through, even if I had been disposed to do so. But I cannot refrain from referring to one or two documents, which have fallen in my way since this debate began. I read, sir, from the Olive Branch of Matthew Carey, in which are collected "the actings and doings" of the peace party of New England, during the continuance of the embargo and the war. I know the senator from Massachusetts will respect the high authority of his political friend and fellow-laborer in the great cause of "domestic industry."

In p. 301, et seq., 309 of this work, is a detailed account of the measures adopted in Massachusetts during the war, for the express purpose of embarrassing the financial operations of the government, by preventing loans, and thereby driving our rulers from their seats, and forcing the country into a dishonorable peace. It appears that the Boston banks commenced an operation, by which a run was to be made upon all the banks to the south; at the same time stopping their own discounts; the effect of which was to produce a sudden and most alarming diminution of the circulating medium, and universal distress over the whole country — "a distress which they failed not to attribute to the unholy war."

To such an extent was this system carried, that it appears, from a statement of the condition of the Boston banks, made up in January, 1814, that with nearly $5,000,000 of specie in their vaults, they had but $2,000,000 of bills in circulation. It is added by Carey, that at this very time an extensive trade was carried on in British government bills, for which specie was sent to Canada, for the payment of the British troops, then laying waste our northern frontier; and this too at the very moment when New England ships, sailing under British licenses, (a trade declared to be lawful by the courts both of Great Britain and Massachusetts,†) were supplying with provisions those very armies destined for the invasion of our own shores. Sir, the author of the Olive Branch, with a

---

* In answer to an address of Governor Eustis, denouncing the conduct of the peace party during the war, the House of Representatives of Massachusetts, in June, 1823, say, " The change of the political sentiments evinced in the late elections forms indeed a new era in the history of our commonwealth. It is the triumph of reason over passion; of patriotism over party spirit. Massachusetts has returned to her first love, and is no longer a stranger in the Union. We rejoice that though, during the last war, such measures were adopted in this state as occasioned double sacrifice of treasure and of life, covered the friends of the nation with humiliation and mourning, and fixed a stain on the page of our history, a redeeming spirit has at length arisen, to take away our reproach, and restore to us our good name, our rank among our sister states, and our just influence in the Union.

" Though we would not renew contentions, or irritate wantonly, we believe that there are cases when it is necessary we should 'wound to heal.' And we consider it among the first duties of the friends of our national government, on this return of power, to disavow the unwarrantable course pursued by this state, during the late war, and to hold up the measures of that period as beacons; that the present and succeeding generations may shun that career which must inevitably terminate in the destruction of the individual or party who pursues it; and may learn the important lesson, that, in all times, the path of duty is the path of safety; and that it is never dangerous to rally around the standard of our country."

† 2d Dodson's Admiralty Reports, 48. 13th Mass. Reports, 26

holy indignation, denounces these acts as "treasonable;" "giving aid and comfort to the enemy." I shall not follow his example. But I will ask, With what justice or propriety can the south be accused of disloyalty from that quarter? If we had any evidence that the senator from Massachusetts had admonished his brethren then, he might, with a better grace, assume the office of admonishing us now.

When I look at the measures adopted in Boston, at that day, to deprive the government of the necessary means for carrying on the war, and think of the success and the consequences of these measures, I feel my pride, as an American, humbled in the dust. Hear, sir, the language of that day. I read from pages 301 and 302 of the Olive Branch. "Let no man who wishes to continue the war, by active means, by vote, or lending money, dare to prostrate himself at the altar on the fast day." "Will federalists subscribe to the loan? Will they lend money to our national rulers? It is impossible. First, because of principle, and secondly, because of principal and interest." "Do not prevent the abusers of their trust from becoming bankrupt. Do not prevent them from becoming odious to the public, and being replaced by better men." "Any federalist who lends money to government must go and shake hands with James Madison, and claim fellowship with Felix Grundy." (I beg pardon of my honorable friend from Tennessee—but he is in good company. I had thought it was "James Madison, Felix Grundy, and the devil.") Let him no more "call himself a federalist, and a friend to his country: he will be called by others infamous," &c.

Sir, the spirit of the people sunk under these appeals. Such was the effect produced by them on the public mind, that the very agents of the government (as appears from their public advertisements, now before me) could not obtain loans without a pledge that "the names of the subscribers should not be known." Here are the advertisements: "The names of all subscribers" (say Gilbert and Dean, the brokers employed by government) "shall be known only to the undersigned." As if those who came forward to aid their country, in the hour of her utmost need, were engaged in some dark and foul conspiracy, they were assured "that their names should not be known." Can any thing show more conclusively the unhappy state of public feeling which prevailed at that day than this single fact? Of the same character with these measures was the conduct of Massachusetts in withholding her militia from the service of the United States, and devising measures for withdrawing her quota of the taxes, thereby attempting, not merely to cripple the resources of the country, but actually depriving the government (as far as depended upon her) of all the means of carrying on the war—of the bone, and muscle, and sinews of war—"of man and steel—the soldier and his sword." But it seems Massachusetts was to reserve her resources for herself—she was to defend and protect her own shores. And how was that duty performed? In some places on the coast neutrality was declared, and the enemy was suffered to invade the soil of Massachusetts, and allowed to occupy her territory until the peace, without one effort to rescue it from his grasp. Nay, more—while our own government and our rulers were considered as enemies, the troops of the enemy were treated like friends—the most intimate commercial relations were established with them, and maintained up to the peace. At this dark period of our national affairs where was the senator from Massachusetts? How were his political associates employed? "Calculating the value of the Union?"

Yes, sir, that was the propitious moment, when our country stood alone, the last hope of the world, struggling for her existence against the colossal power of Great Britain, " concentrated in one mighty effort to crush us at a blow ; " that was the chosen hour to revive the grand scheme of building up "a great northern confederacy" — a scheme which, it is stated in the work before me, had its origin as far back as the year 1796, and which appears never to have been entirely abandoned.

In the language of the writers of that day, (1796,) " rather than have a constitution such as the anti-federalists were contending for, (such as we are now contending for,) the Union ought to be dissolved ; " and to prepare the way for that measure, the same methods were resorted to then that have always been relied on for that purpose, exciting prejudice against the south. Yes, sir, our northern brethren were then told, "that if the negroes were good for food, their southern masters would claim the right to destroy them at pleasure." (Olive Branch, p. 267.) Sir, in 1814, all these topics were revived. Again we hear of " a northern confederacy." " The slave states by themselves ; " " the mountains are the natural boundary ; " we want neither " the counsels nor the power of the west," &c., &c. The papers teemed with accusations against the *south* and the *west*, and the calls for a dissolution of all connection with them were loud and strong. I cannot consent to go through the disgusting details. But to show the height to which the spirit of disaffection was carried, I will take you to the temple of the living God, and show you *that sacred place,* which should be devoted to the extension of " peace on earth and good will towards men," where " *one day's truce* ought surely to be allowed to the dissensions and animosities of mankind," converted into *a fierce arena of political strife,* where, from the lips of the priest, standing between the horns of the altar, there went forth the most *terrible denunciations* against all who should be true to their country in the hour of her utmost need.

" If you do not wish," said a reverend clergyman, in a sermon preached in Boston, on the 23d July, 1812, " to become the slaves of those who own slaves, and who are themselves the slaves of French slaves, you must either, *in the language of the day,* CUT THE CONNECTION, or so far alter the national compact as to insure to yourselves a due share in the government." (Olive Branch, p. 319.) " The Union," says the same writer, (p. 320,) " has been long since virtually dissolved, and it is full time that this part of the disunited states should take care of itself."

Another reverend gentleman, pastor of a church at Medford, (p. 321,) issues his anathema — " LET HIM STAND ACCURSED " — against all, all who, by their " personal services," for " loans of money," " conversation," or " writing," or " influence," give countenance or support to the unrighteous war, in the following terms : " That man is an accomplice in the wickedness — he loads his conscience with the blackest crimes — he brings the guilt of blood upon his soul, and in the sight of God and his law, *he is a* MURDERER."

One or two more quotations, sir, and I shall have done. A reverend doctor of divinity, the pastor of a church at Byfield, Massachusetts, on the 7th of April, 1814, thus addresses his flock, (p. 321 :) " The Israelites became weary of yielding the fruit of their labor to pamper their splendid tyrants. They left their political woes. THEY SEPARATED ; where is our Moses ? Where the rod of his miracles ? Where is our Aaron ? Alas ! no voice from the burning bush has directed them here."

"We must trample on the mandates of despotism, or remain slaves forever," (p. 322.) "You must drag the chains of Virginian despotism, unless you discover some other mode of escape." . "Those Western States which have been violent for this abominable war — those states which have thirsted for blood — God has given them blood to drink," (p. 323.) Mr. President, I can go no further. The records of the day are full of such sentiments, issued from the press, spoken in public assemblies, poured out from the sacred desk. God forbid, sir, that I should charge the people of Massachusetts with participating in these sentiments. The south and the west had there their friends — men who stood by their country, though encompassed all around by their enemies. The senator from Massachusetts (Mr. Silsbee) was one of them; the senator from Connecticut (Mr. Foot) was another; and there are others now on this floor. The sentiments I have read were the sentiments of a party embracing the political associates of the gentleman from Massachusetts. If they could only be found in the columns of a newspaper, in a few occasional pamphlets, issued by men of intemperate feeling, I should not consider them as affording any evidence of the opinions even of the peace party of New England. But, sir, they were the common language of that day; they pervaded the whole land; they were issued from the legislative hall, from the pulpit, and the press. Our books are full of them; and there is no man who now hears me but knows that they were the sentiments of a party, by whose members they were promulgated. Indeed, no evidence of this would seem to be required beyond the fact that such sentiments found their way even into the pulpits of New England. What must be the state of public opinion, where any respectable clergyman would venture to preach, and to print, sermons containing the sentiments I have quoted? I doubt not the piety or moral worth of these gentlemen. I am told they were respectable and pious men. But they were men, and they "kindled in a common blaze." And now, sir, I must be suffered to remark that, at this awful and melancholy period of our national history, the gentleman from Massachusetts, who now manifests so great a devotion to the Union, and so much anxiety lest it should be endangered from the south, was "with his brethren in Israel." He saw all these things passing before his eyes — he heard these sentiments uttered all around him. I do not charge that gentleman with any participation in these acts, or with approving of these sentiments.

But I will ask, why, if he was animated by the same sentiments then which he now professes, if he can "augur disunion at a distance, and snuff up rebellion in every tainted breeze," why did he not, at that day, exert his great talents and acknowledged influence with the political associates by whom he was surrounded, and who then, as now, looked up to him for guidance and direction, in allaying this general excitement, in pointing out to his deluded friends the value of the Union, in instructing them that, instead of looking "to some prophet to lead them out of the land of Egypt," they should become reconciled to their brethren, and unite with them in the support of a just and necessary war? Sir, the gentleman must excuse me for saying, that if the records of our country afforded any evidence that he had pursued such a course, then, if we could find it recorded in the history of those times, that, like the immortal Dexter, he had breasted that mighty torrent which was sweeping before it all that was great and valuable in our political institutions — if like him he had stood by his country in opposition to his party, sir, we would, like little children, listen to his precepts, and abide by his counsels.

As soon as the public mind was sufficiently prepared for the measure, the celebrated Hartford Convention was got up; not as the act of a few unauthorized individuals, but by authority of the legislature of Massachusetts; and, as has been shown by the able historian of that convention, in accordance with the views and wishes of the party of which it was the organ. Now, sir, I do not desire to call in question the motives of the gentlemen who composed that assembly. I knew many of them to be in private life accomplished and honorable men, and I doubt not there were some among them who did not perceive the dangerous tendency of their proceedings. I will even go further, and say, that if the authors of the Hartford Convention believed that "gross, deliberate, and palpable violations of the constitution" had taken place, utterly destructive of their rights and interests, I should be the last man to deny their right to resort to any constitutional measures for redress. But, sir, in any view of the case, the time when and the circumstances under which that convention assembled, as well as the measures recommended, render their conduct, in my opinion, wholly indefensible. Let us contemplate, for a moment, the spectacle then exhibited to the view of the world. I will not go over the disasters of the war, nor describe the difficulties in which the government was involved. It will be recollected that its credit was nearly gone, Washington had fallen, the whole coast was blockaded, and an immense force, collected in the West Indies, was about to make a descent, which it was supposed we had no means of resisting. In this awful state of our public affairs, when the government seemed almost to be tottering on its base, when Great Britain, relieved from all her other enemies, had proclaimed her purpose of "reducing us to unconditional submission," we beheld the peace party of New England (in the language of the work before us) pursuing a course calculated to do more injury to their country, and to render England more effective service than all her armies." Those who could not find it in their hearts to rejoice at our victories sang Te Deum at the King's Chapel in Boston, for the restoration of the Bourbons. Those who could not consent to illuminate their dwellings for the capture of the Guerriere could give no visible tokens of their joy at the fall of Detroit. The "beacon fires" of their hills were lighted up, not for the encouragement of their friends, but as signals to the enemy; and in the gloomy hours of midnight, the very lights burned blue. Such were the dark and portentous signs of the times, which ushered into being the renowned Hartford Convention. That convention met, and, from their proceedings, it appears that their chief object was to keep back the men and money of New England from the service of the Union, and to effect radical changes in the government — changes that can never be effected without a dissolution of the Union.

Let us now, sir, look at their proceedings. I read from " A Short Account of the Hartford Convention," (written by one of its members,) a very rare book, of which I was fortunate enough, a few years ago, to obtain a copy. [Here Mr. H. read from the proceedings.*]

---

* It appears at p. 6 of the "Account" that, by a vote of the House of Representatives of Massachusetts, (260 to 290,) delegates to this convention were ordered to be appointed to consult upon the subject " of their public grievances and concerns," and upon "the best means of preserving their resources," and for procuring a revision of the constitution of the United States, "more effectually to secure the support and attachment of all the people, by placing all upon the basis of fair representation."
The convention assembled at Hartford on the 15th December, 1814. On the **next day** it was

It is unnecessary to trace the matter further, or to ask what would
have been the next chapter in this history, if the measures recommended
had been carried into effect; and if, with the men and money of New
England withheld from the government of the United States, she had
been withdrawn from the war; if New Orleans had fallen into the hands
of the enemy; and if, without troops and almost destitute of money, the
Southern and the Western States had been thrown upon their own resources, for the prosecution of the war, and the recovery of New
Orleans.

Sir, whatever may have been the issue of the contest, the Union must
have been dissolved. But a wise and just Providence, which "shapes
our ends, roughhew them as we will," gave us the victory, and crowned
our efforts with a glorious peace. The ambassadors of Hartford were
seen retracing their steps from Washington, "the bearers of the glad
tidings of great joy." Courage and patriotism triumphed—the country
was saved—the Union was preserved. And are we, Mr. President, who
stood by our country then, who threw open our coffers, who bared our
bosoms, who freely perilled all in that conflict, to be reproached with
want of attachment to the Union? If, sir, we are to have lessons of
patriotism read to us, they must come from a different quarter. The
senator from Massachusetts, who is now so sensitive on all subjects connected with the Union, seems to have a memory forgetful of the political

Resolved, That the most inviolable secrecy shall be observed by each member of
this convention, including the secretary, as to all propositions, debates, and proceedings
thereof, until this injunction shall be suspended or altered.

On the 24th of December, the committee appointed to prepare and report a general
project of such measures as may be proper for the convention to adopt, reported,
among other things,—

"1. That it was expedient to recommend to the legislatures of the states the adoption of the most effectual and decisive measures to protect the militia of the states from
the usurpations contained in these proceedings." [The proceedings of Congress and
the executive, in relation to the militia and the war.]

"2. That it was expedient also to prepare a statement, exhibiting the necessity
which the improvidence and inability of the general government have imposed upon
the states of providing for their own defence, and the impossibility of their dis-
charging this duty, and at the same time fulfilling the requisitions of the general
government, and also to recommend to the legislatures of the several states to make
provision for mutual defence, and to make an earnest application to the government
of the United States, with a view to some arrangement whereby the states may be
enabled to retain a portion of the taxes levied by Congress, for the purposes of self-
defence, and for the reimbursement of expenses already incurred on account of the
United States.

"3. That it is expedient to recommend to the several state legislatures certain
amendments to the constitution, viz.,—

"That the power to declare or make war, by the Congress of the United States, be
restricted.

"That it is expedient to attempt to make provision for restraining Congress in the
exercise of an unlimited power to make new states, and admit them into the Union.

"That an amendment be proposed respecting slave representation and slave taxation."

On the 29th of December, 1814, it was proposed "that the capacity of naturalized
citizens to hold offices of trust, honor, or profit ought to be restrained," &c.

The subsequent proceedings are not given at large. But it seems that the report
of the committee was adopted, and also a recommendation of certain measures (of the
character of which we are not informed) to the states for their mutual defence; and
having voted that the injunction of secrecy, in regard to all the debates and proceedings of the convention, (except so far as relates to the report finally adopted,) be continued, the convention adjourned *sine die*, but, as it was supposed, to meet again when
circumstances should require it.

events that have passed away. I must therefore refresh his recollection a little further on these subjects. The history of disunion has been written by one whose authority stands too high with the American people to be questioned; I mean Thomas Jefferson. I know not how the gentleman may receive this authority. When that great and good man occupied the presidential chair, I believe he commanded no portion of the gentleman's respect.

I hold in my hand a celebrated pamphlet on the embargo, in which language is held, in relation to Mr. Jefferson, which my respect for his memory will prevent me from reading, unless any gentleman should call for it. But the senator from Massachusetts has since joined in singing hosannas to his name; he has assisted at his apotheosis, and has fixed him as "a brilliant star in the clear upper sky." I hope, therefore, he is now prepared to receive with deference and respect the high authority of Mr. Jefferson. In the fourth volume of his Memoirs, which has just issued from the press, we have the following history of disunion from the pen of that illustrious statesman : " Mr. Adams called on me pending the embargo, and while endeavors were making to obtain its repeal : he spoke of the dissatisfaction of the eastern portion of our confederacy with the restraints of the embargo then existing, and their restlessness under it ; that there was nothing which might not be attempted to rid themselves of it ; that he had information of the most unquestionable authority, that certain citizens of the Eastern States (I think he named Massachusetts particularly) were in negotiation with agents of the British government, the object of which was an agreement that the New England States should take no further part in the war (the commercial war, the 'war of restrictions,' as it was called) then going on, and that, without formally declaring their separation from the Union, they should withdraw from all aid and obedience to them, &c. From that moment," says Mr. J., " I saw the necessity of abandoning it, [the embargo,] and, instead of effecting our purpose by this peaceful measure, we must fight it out or break the Union." In another letter, Mr. Jefferson adds, " I doubt whether a single fact known to the world will carry as clear conviction to it of the correctness of our knowledge of the treasonable views of the federal party of that day, as that disclosed by this, the most nefarious and daring attempt to dissever the Union, of which the Hartford Convention was a subsequent chapter ; and both of these having failed, consolidation becomes the fourth chapter of the next book of their history. But this opens with a vast accession of strength, from their younger recruits, who, having nothing in them of the feelings and principles of '76, now look to a single and splendid government, &c., riding and ruling over the plundered ploughman and beggared yeomanry." (vol. iv. pp. 419, 422.)

The last chapter, says Mr. Jefferson, of that history, is to be found in the conduct of those who are endeavoring to bring about consolidation ; ay, sir, that very consolidation for which the gentleman from Massachusetts is contending — the exercise by the federal government of powers not delegated in relation to "internal improvements " and " the protection of manufactures.'' And why, sir, does Mr. Jefferson consider consolidation as leading directly to disunion ? Because he knew that the exercise, by the federal government, of the powers contended for, would make this "a government without limitation of powers," the submission to which he considered as a greater evil than disunion itself. There i one chapter in this history, however, which Mr. Jefferson has not filled up; and I must therefore supply the deficiency. It is to be found in the protests made by New England against the acquisition of Louisiana. In relation to that subject, the New England doctrine is thus laid down by one of her learned doctors of that day, now a doctor of laws, at the head of the great literary institution of the east; I mean Josiah Quincy, president of Harvard College. I quote from the speech delivered by that gentleman on the floor of Congress, on the occasion of the admission of Louisiana into the Union.

"Mr. Quincy repeated and justified a remark he had made, which, to save all misapprehension, he had committed to writing, in the following words: If this bill passes, it is my deliberate opinion that it is virtually a dissolution of the Union; that it will free the states from their moral obligation; and as it will be the right of all, so it will be the duty of some, to prepare for a separation, amicably if they can, violently if they must."

Mr. President, I wish it to be distinctly understood, that all the remarks I have made on this subject are intended to be exclusively applied to a party, which I have described as the "peace party of New England"— embracing the political associates of the senator from Massachusetts — a party which controlled the operations of that state during the embargo and the war, and who are justly chargeable with all the measures I have reprobated. Sir, nothing has been further from my thoughts than to impeach the character or conduct of the people of New England. For their steady habits and hardy virtues I trust I entertain a becoming respect. I fully subscribe to the truth of the description given before the revolution, by one whose praise is the highest eulogy, "that the perseverance of Holland, the activity of France, and the dexterous and firm sagacity of English enterprise, have been more than equalled by this recent people." Hardy, enterprising, sagacious, industrious, and moral, the people of New England of the present day are worthy of their ancestors. Still less, Mr. President, has it been my intention to say any thing that could be construed into a want of respect for that party, who, trampling on all narrow, sectional feeling, have been true to their principles in the worst of times; I mean the democracy of New England.

Sir, I will declare that, highly as I appreciate the democracy of the south, I consider even higher praise to be due to the democracy of New England, who have maintained their principles "through good and through evil report," who, at every period of our national history, have stood up manfully for "their country, their whole country, and nothing but their country." In the great political revolution of '98, they were found united with the democracy of the south, marching under the banner of the constitution, led on by the patriarch of liberty, in search of the land of political promise, which they lived not only to behold, but to possess and to enjoy. Again, sir, in the darkest and most gloomy period of the war, when our country stood single-handed against "the conquerer of the conquerers of the world," when all about and around them was dark and dreary, disastrous and discouraging, they stood a Spartan band in that narrow pass, where the honor of their country was to be defended, or to find its grave. And in the last great struggle, involving, as we believe, the very existence of the principle of popular sovereignty where were the democracy of New England? Where they always have been found, sir, struggling side by side, with their brethren of the south and the west, for popular rights, and assisting in that glorious triumph, by which the man of the people was elevated to the highest office in their gift.

Who, then, Mr. President, are the true friends of the Union? Those who would confine the federal government strictly within the limits prescribed by the constitution; who would preserve to the states and the people all powers not expressly delegated; who would make this a federal and not a national Union, and who, administering the government in a spirit of equal justice, would make it a blessing, and not a curse. And who are its enemies? Those who are in favor of consolidation; who are constantly stealing power from the states, and adding strength to the federal government; who, assuming an unwarrantable jurisdiction over the states and the people, undertake to regulate the whole industry and capital of the country. But, sir, of all descriptions of men, I consider those as the worst enemies of the Union, who sacrifice the equal rights which belong to every member of the confederacy to combinations of interested majorities, for personal or political objects. But the gentleman apprehends no evil from the dependence of the states on the federal government; he can see no danger of corruption from the influence of money or of patronage. Sir, I know that it is supposed to be a wise saying that "patronage is a source of weakness;" and in support of that maxim, it has been said, that "every ten appointments make a hundred enemies." But I am rather inclined to think, with the eloquent and sagacious orator now reposing on his laurels on the banks of the Roanoke, that "the power of conferring favors creates a crowd of dependants;" he gave a forcible illustration of the truth of the remark, when he told us of the effect of holding up the savory morsel to the eager eyes of the hungry hounds gathered around his door. It mattered not whether the gift was bestowed on Towzer or Sweetlips, "Tray, Blanch, or Sweetheart;" while held in suspense, they were all governed by a nod, and when the morsel was bestowed, the expectation of the favors of to-morrow kept up the subjection of to-day.

The senator from Massachusetts, in denouncing what he is pleased to call the Carolina doctrine, has attempted to throw ridicule upon the idea that a state has any constitutional remedy, by the exercise of its sovereign authority, against "a gross, palpable, and deliberate violation of the constitution." He calls it "an idle" or "a ridiculous notion," or something to that effect, and added, that it would make the Union a "mere rope of sand." Now, sir, as the gentleman has not condescended to enter into any examination of the question, and has been satisfied with throwing the weight of his authority into the scale, I do not deem it necessary to do more than to throw into the opposite scale the authority on which South Carolina relies; and there, for the present, I am perfectly willing to leave the controversy. The South Carolina doctrine, that is to say, the doctrine contained in an exposition reported by a committee of the legislature in December, 1828, and published by their authority, is the good old republican doctrine of '98 — the doctrine of the celebrated "Virginia Resolutions" of that year, and of "Madison's Report" of '99. It will be recollected that the legislature of Virginia, in December, '98, took into consideration the alien and sedition laws, then considered by all republicans as a gross violation of the constitution of the United States, and on that day passed, among others, the following resolutions: —

"The General Assembly doth explicitly and peremptorily declare, that

3

it views the powers of the federal government, as resulting from the compact to which the states are parties, as limited by the plain sense and intention of the instrument constituting that compact, as no further valid than they are authorized by the grants enumerated in that compact; and that in case of a deliberate, palpable, and dangerous exercise of other powers not granted by the said compact, the states who are parties thereto have the right, and are in duty bound, to interpose for arresting the progress of the evil, and for maintaining, within their respective limits, the authorities, rights, and liberties appertaining to them."

In addition to the above resolution, the General Assembly of Virginia "appealed to the other states, in the confidence that they would concur with that commonwealth, that the acts aforesaid [the alien and sedition laws] are unconstitutional, and that the necessary and proper measures would be taken by each for coöperating with Virginia in maintaining unimpaired the authorities, rights, and liberties reserved to the states respectively, or to the people."

The legislatures of several of the New England States, having, contrary to the expectation of the legislature of Virginia, expressed their dissent from these doctrines, the subject came up again for consideration during the session of 1799, 1800, when it was referred to a select committee, by whom was made that celebrated report which is familiarly known as "Madison's Report," and which deserves to last as long as the constitution itself. In that report, which was subsequently adopted by the legislature, the whole subject was deliberately reexamined, and the objections urged against the Virginia doctrines carefully considered. The result was, that the legislature of Virginia reaffirmed all the principles laid down in the resolutions of 1798, and issued to the world that admirable report which has stamped the character of Mr. Madison as the preserver of that constitution which he had contributed so largely to create and establish. I will here quote from Mr. Madison's report one or two passages which bear more immediately on the point in controversy. "The resolutions, having taken this view of the federal compact, proceed to infer 'that in case of a deliberate, palpable, and dangerous exercise of other powers, not granted by the said compact, the states who are parties thereto have the right, and are in duty bound, to interpose for arresting the progress of the evil, and for maintaining, within their respective limits, the authorities, rights, and liberties appertaining to them.' "

" It appears to your committee to be a plain principle, founded in common sense, illustrated by common practice, and essential to the nature of compacts, that, where resort can be had to no tribunal superior to the authority of the parties, the parties themselves must be the rightful judges in the last resort, whether the bargain made has been pursued or violated. The constitution of the United States was formed by the sanction of the states, given by each in its sovereign capacity. It adds to the stability and dignity, as well as to the authority, of the constitution, that it rests upon this legitimate and solid foundation. The states, then, being the parties to the constitutional compact, and in their sovereign capacity, it follows of necessity that there can be no tribunal above their authority, to decide, in the last resort, whether the compact made by them be violated, and consequently that, as the parties to it, they must themselves decide, in the last resort, such questions as may be of sufficient magnitude to require their interposition."

" The resolution has guarded against any misapprehension of its object by expressly requiring for such an interposition 'the case of a deliberate, palpable, and dangerous breach of the constitution, by the exercise of powers not granted by it.' It must be a case, not of a light and transient nature, but of a nature dangerous to the great purposes for which the constitution was established.

" But the resolution has done more than guard against misconstruction, by expressly referring to cases of a deliberate, palpable, and dangerous nature. It specifies the object of the interposition, which it contemplates, to be solely that of arresting the progress of the evil of usurpation, and of maintaining the authorities, rights, and liberties appertaining to the states, as parties to the constitution.

" From this view of the resolution, it would seem inconceivable that it can incur any just disapprobation from those who, laying aside all momentary impressions, and recollecting the genuine source and object of the federal constitution, shall candidly and accurately interpret the meaning of the General Assembly. If the deliberate exercise of dangerous powers, palpably withheld by the constitution, could not justify the parties to it in interposing even so far as to arrest the progress of the evil, and thereby to preserve the constitution itself, as well as to provide for the safety of the parties to it, there would be an end to all relief from usurped power, and a direct subversion of the rights specified or recognized under all the state constitutions, as well as a plain denial of the fundamental principles on which our independence itself was declared."

But, sir, our authorities do not stop here. The state of Kentucky responded to Virginia, and on the 10th of November, 1798, adopted those celebrated resolutions, well known to have been penned by the author of the Declaration of American Independence. In those resolutions, the legislature of Kentucky declare, "that the government created by this compact was not made the exclusive or final judge of the extent of the powers delegated to itself, since that would have made its discretion, and not the constitution, the measure of its powers; but that, as in all other cases of compact among parties having no common judge, each party has an equal right to judge, for itself, as well of infractions as of the mode and measure of redress."

At the ensuing session of the legislature, the subject was reëxamined, and on the 14th of ·November, 1799, the resolutions of the preceding year were deliberately reaffirmed, and it was, among other things, solemnly declared, —

" That, if those who administer the general government be permitted to transgress the limits fixed by that compact, by a total disregard to the special delegations of power therein contained, an annihilation of the state governments, and the erection upon their ruins of a general consolidated government, will be the inevitable consequence. That the principles of construction contended for by sundry of the state legislatures, that the general government is the exclusive judge of the extent of the powers delegated to it, stop nothing short of despotism ; since the discretion of those who administer the government, and not the constitution, would be the measure of their powers. That the several states who formed that instrument, being sovereign and independent, have the un questionable right to judge of its infraction, and that a nullification, by those sovereignties, of all unauthorized acts done under color of that in strument, is the rightful remedy."

Time and experience confirmed Mr. Jefferson's opinion on this all important point. In the year 1821, he expressed himself in this emphatic manner: "It is a fatal heresy to suppose that either our state governments are superior to the federal, or the federal to the state; neither is authorized literally to decide which belongs to itself or its copartner in government; in differences of opinion, between their different sets of public servants, the appeal is to neither, but to their employers peaceably assembled by their representatives in convention." The opinion of Mr. Jefferson on this subject has been so repeatedly and so solemnly expressed, that they may be said to have been among the most fixed and settled convictions of his mind.

In the protest prepared by him for the legislature of Virginia, in December, 1825, in respect to the powers exercised by the federal government in relation to the tariff and internal improvements, which he declares to be "usurpations of the powers retained by the states, mere interpolations into the compact, and direct infractions of it," he solemnly reasserts all the principles of the Virginia Resolutions of '98, protests against "these acts of the federal branch of the government as null and void, and declares that, although Virginia would consider a dissolution of the Union as among the greatest calamities that could befall them, yet it is not the greatest. There is one yet greater — submission to a government of unlimited powers. It is only when the hope of this shall become absolutely desperate, that further forbearance could not be indulged."

In his letter to Mr. Giles, written about the same time, he says, —

"I see as you do, and with the deepest affliction, the rapid strides with which the federal branch of our government is advancing towards the usurpation of all the rights reserved to the states, and the consolidation in itself of all powers, foreign and domestic, and that too by constructions which leave no limits to their powers, &c. Under the power to regulate commerce, they assume, indefinitely, that also over agriculture and manufactures, &c. Under the authority to establish post roads, they claim that of cutting down mountains for the construction of roads, and digging canals, &c. And what is our resource for the preservation of the constitution? Reason and argument? You might as well reason and argue with the marble columns encircling them, &c. Are we then to stand to our arms with the hot-headed Georgian? No; [and I say no, and South Carolina has said no;] that must be the last resource. We must have patience and long endurance with our brethren, &c., and separate from our companions only when the sole alternatives left are a dissolution of our Union with them, or submission to a government without limitation of powers. Between these two evils, when we must make a choice, there can be no hesitation."

Such, sir, are the high and imposing authorities in support of "the Carolina doctrine," which is, in fact, the doctrine of the Virginia Resolutions of 1798.

Sir, at that day the whole country was divided on this very question. It formed the line of demarcation between the federal and republican parties; and the great political revolution which then took place turned upon the very questions involved in these resolutions. That question was decided by the people, and by that decision the constitution was, in the emphatic language of Mr. Jefferson, "saved at its last gasp." I should suppose, sir, it would require more self-respect than any gentleman here would be willing to assume, to treat lightly doctrines derived from such high resources. Resting on authority like this, I will ask gentlemen whether South Carolina has not manifested a high regard for the Union, when, under a tyranny ten times more grievous than the alien and sedition laws, she has hitherto gone no further than to petition, remonstrate, and to solemnly protest against a series of measures which she believes to be wholly unconstitutional and utterly destructive of her interests. Sir, South Carolina has not gone one step further than Mr. Jefferson himself was disposed to go, in relation to the present subject of our present complaints—not a step further than the statesmen from New England were disposed to go, under similar circumstances; no further than the senator from Massachusetts himself once considered as within "the limits of a constitutional opposition." The doctrine that it is the right of a state to judge of the violations of the constitution on the part of the federal government, and to protect her citizens from the operations of unconstitutional laws, was held by the enlightened citizens of Boston, who assembled in Faneuil Hall, on the 25th of January, 1809. They state, in that celebrated memorial, that "they looked only to the state legislature, who were competent to devise relief against the unconstitutional acts of the general government. That your power (say they) is adequate to that object, is evident from the organization of the confederacy."

A distinguished senator from one of the New England States, (Mr. Hillhouse,) in a speech delivered here, on a bill for enforcing the embargo, declared, "I feel myself bound in conscience to declare, (lest the blood of those who shall fall in the execution of this measure shall be on my head,) that I consider this to be an act which directs a mortal blow at the liberties of my country — an act containing unconstitutional provisions, to which the people are not bound to submit, and to which, in my opinion, they will not submit."

And the senator from Massachusetts himself, in a speech delivered on the same subject in the other house, said, "This opposition is constitutional and legal; it is also conscientious. It rests on settled and sober conviction, that such policy is destructive to the interests of the people, and dangerous to the being of government. The experience of every day confirms these sentiments. Men who act from such motives are not to be discouraged by trifling obstacles, nor awed by any dangers. They know the limit of constitutional opposition; up to that limit, at their own discretion, they will walk, and walk fearlessly." How "the being of the government" was to be endangered by "constitutional opposition" to the embargo, I leave to the gentleman to explain.

Thus it will be seen, Mr. President, that the South Carolina doctrine is the republican doctrine of '98 — that it was promulgated by the fathers of the faith — that it was maintained by Virginia and Kentucky in the worst of times — that it constituted the very pivot on which the political revolution of that day turned — that it embraces the very principles, the triumph of which, at that time, saved the constitution at its last gasp, and which New England statesmen were not unwilling to adopt, when they believed themselves to be the victims of unconstitutional legislation. Sir, as to the doctrine that the federal government is the exclusive judge of the extent as well as the limitations of its powers, it seems to me to be utterly subversive of the sovereignty and independence of the states. It makes but little difference, in my estimation, whether Congress or the Supreme Court are invested with this power. If the federal government, in all, or any, of its departments, is to prescribe the limits of its own authority, and the states are bound to submit to the decision, and are not to be allowed to examine and decide for themselves, when the barriers of the constitution shall be overleaped, this is practically "a government without limitation of powers." The states are at once reduced to mere petty corporations, and the people are entirely at your mercy. I have but one word more to add. In all the efforts that have been made by South Carolina to resist the unconstitutional laws which Congress has extended over them, she has kept steadily in view the preservation of the Union, by the only means by which she believes it can be long preserved — a firm, manly, and steady resistance against usurpation. The measures of the federal government have, it is true, prostrated her interests, and will soon involve the whole south in irretrievable ruin. But even this evil, great as it is, is not the chief ground of our complaints. It is the principle involved in the contest — a principle which, substituting the discretion of Congress for the limitations of the constitution, brings the states and the people to the feet of the federal government, and leaves them nothing they can call their own. Sir, if the measures of the federal government were less oppressive, we should still strive against this usurpation. The south is acting on a principle she has always held sacred — resistance to unauthorized taxation. These, sir, are the principles which induced the immortal Hampden to resist the payment of a tax of twenty shillings. Would twenty shillings have ruined his fortune? No! but the payment of half twenty shillings, on the principle on which it was demanded, would have made him a slave. Sir, if acting on these high motives — if animated by that ardent love of liberty which has always been the most prominent trait in the southern character — we should be hurried beyond the bounds of a cold and calculating prudence, who is there, with one noble and generous sentiment in his bosom, that would not be disposed, in the language of Burke, to exclaim, " You must pardon something to the spirit of liberty"?

MR. WEBSTER'S SPEECH.

In Senate, January 26, 1830.

FOLLOWING Mr. HAYNE in the debate, Mr. WEBSTER addressed the Senate as follows : —

Mr. PRESIDENT : When the mariner has been tossed, for many days, in thick weather, and on an unknown sea, he naturally avails himself of the first pause in the storm, the earliest glance of the sun, to take his latitude, and ascertain how far the elements have driven him from his true course. Let us imitate this prudence, and before we float farther, refer to the point from which we departed, that we may at least be able to conjecture where we now are. I ask for the reading of the resolution.

[The secretary read the resolution, as follows : —

"*Resolved*, That the committee on public lands be instructed to inquire and report the quantity of the public lands remaining unsold within each state and territory, and whether it be expedient to limit, for a certain period, the sales of the public lands to such lands only as have heretofore been offered for sale, and are now subject to entry at the minimum price. And, also, whether the office of surveyor general, and some of the land offices, may not be abolished without detriment to the public interest; or whether it be expedient to adopt measures to hasten the sales, and extend more rapidly the surveys of the public lands."]

We have thus heard, sir, what the resolution is, which is actually before us for consideration; and it will readily occur to every one that it is almost the only subject about which something has not been said in the speech, running through two days, by which the Senate has been now entertained by the gentleman from South Carolina. Every topic in the wide range of our public affairs, whether past or present, — every thing, general or local, whether belonging to national politics or party politics, — seems to have attracted more or less of the honorable member's attention, save only the resolution before us. He has spoken of every thing but the public lands. They have escaped his notice. To that subject, in all his excursions, he has not paid even the cold respect of a passing glance.

When this debate, sir, was to be resumed, on Thursday morning, it so happened that it would have been convenient for me to be elsewhere. The honorable member, however, did not incline to put off the discussion to another day. He had a shot, he said, to return, and he wished to discharge it. That shot, sir, which it was kind thus to inform us was coming, that we might stand out of the way, or prepare ourselves to fall before it, and die with decency, has now been received. Under all advantages, and with expectation awakened by the tone which preceded it, it has been discharged, and has spent its force. It may become me to say no more of its effect than that, if nobody is found, after all, either killed or wounded by it, it is not the first time in the history of human affairs

(37)

that the vigor and success of the war have not quite come up to the lofty and sounding phrase of the manifesto.

The gentleman, sir, in declining to postpone the debate, told the Senate, with the emphasis of his hand upon his heart, that there was something rankling *here,* which he wished to relieve. [Mr. HAYNE rose and disclaimed having used the word *rankling.*] It would not, Mr. President, be safe for the honorable member to appeal to those around him, upon the question whether he did, in fact, make use of that word. But he may have been unconscious of it. At any rate, it is enough that he disclaims it. But still, with or without the use of that particular word, he had yet something *here,* he said, of which he wished to rid himself by an immediate reply. In this respect, sir, I have a great advantage over the honorable gentleman. There is nothing *here,* sir, which gives me the slightest uneasiness; neither fear, nor anger, nor that which is sometimes more troublesome than either, the consciousness of having been in the wrong. There is nothing either originating *here,* or now received here by the gentleman's shot. Nothing original, for I had not the slightest feeling of disrespect or unkindness towards the honorable member. Some passages, it is true, had occurred, since our acquaintance in this body, which I could have wished might have been otherwise; but I had used philosophy, and forgotten them. When the honorable member rose, in his first speech, I paid him the respect of attentive listening; and when he sat down, though surprised, and I must say even astonished, at some of his opinions, nothing was farther from my intention than to commence any personal warfare; and through the whole of the few remarks I made in answer, I avoided, studiously and carefully, every thing which I thought possible to be construed into disrespect. And, sir, while there is thus nothing originating *here,* which I wished at any time, or now wish, to discharge, I must repeat, also, that nothing has been received *here,* which *rankles,* or in any way gives me annoyance. I will not accuse the honorable member of violating the rules of civilized war — I will not say that he poisoned his arrows. But whether his shafts were, or were not, dipped in that which would have caused rankling if they had reached, there was not, as it happened, quite strength enough in the bow to bring them to their mark. If he wishes now to find those shafts, he must look for them elsewhere; they will not be found fixed and quivering in the object at which they were aimed.

The honorable member complained that I had slept on his speech. I must have slept on it, or not slept at all. The moment the honorable member sat down, his friend from Missouri rose, and, with much honeyed commendation of the speech, suggested that the impressions which it had produced were too charming and delightful to be disturbed by other sentiments or other sounds, and proposed that the Senate should adjourn. Would it have been quite amiable in me, sir, to interrupt this excellent good feeling? Must I not have been absolutely malicious, if I could have thrust myself forward to destroy sensations thus pleasing? Was it not much better and kinder, both to sleep upon them myself, and to allow others, also, the pleasure of sleeping upon them? But if it be meant, by sleeping upon his speech, that I took time to prepare a reply to it, it is quite a mistake: owing to other engagements, I could not employ even the interval between the adjournment of the Senate and its meeting the next morning in attention to the subject of this debate. Nevertheless, sir, the mere matter of fact is undoubtedly true — I did sleep on the gentleman's speech, and slept soundly. And I slept equally well on his speech of yesterday, to which I am now replying. It is quite possible that, in this respect also, I possess some advantage over the honorable member, attributable, doubtless, to a cooler temperament on my part; for in truth I slept upon his speeches remarkably well. But the gentleman inquires why he was made the object of such a reply. Why was he singled out? If an attack had been made on the east, he, he assures us, did not begin it — it was the gentleman from Missouri. Sir, I answered the gentleman's speech because I happened to hear it; and because, also, I chose to give an answer to that speech, which, if unanswered, I thought most likely to produce injurious impressions. I did not stop to inquire who was the original drawer of the bill. I found a responsible indorser before me, and it was my purpose to hold him liable, and to bring him to his just responsibility without delay. But, sir, this interrogatory of the honorable member was only introductory to another. He proceeded to ask me whether I had turned upon him in this debate from the consciousness that I should find an overmatch if I ventured on a contest with his friend from Missouri. If, sir, the honorable member, *ex gratia modestiæ*, had chosen thus to defer to his friend, and to pay him a compliment, without intentional disparagement to others, it would have been quite according to the friendly courtesies of debate, and not at all ungrateful to my own feelings. I am not one of those, sir, who esteem any tribute of regard, whether light and occasional, or more serious and deliberate, which may be bestowed on others, as so much unjustly withholden from themselves. But the tone and manner of the gentleman's question forbid me thus to interpret it. I am not at liberty to consider it as nothing more than a civility to his friend. It had an air of taunt and disparagement, a little of the loftiness of asserted superiority, which does not allow me to pass it over without notice. It was put as a question for me to answer, and so put as if it were difficult for me to answer, whether I deemed the member from Missouri an overmatch for myself in debate here. It seems to me, sir, that is extraordinary language, and an extraordinary tone for the discussions of this body.

Matches and overmatches! Those terms are more applicable elsewhere than here, and fitter for other assemblies than this. Sir, the gentleman seems to forget where and what we are. This is a Senate; a senate of equals; of men of individual honor and personal character, and of absolute independence. We know no masters; we acknowledge no dictators. This is a hall for mutual consultation and discussion, not an arena for the exhibition of champions. I offer myself, sir, as a match for no man; I throw the challenge of debate at no man's feet. But, then, sir, since the honorable member has put the question in a manner that calls for an answer, I will give him an answer; and I tell him that, holding myself to be the humblest of the members here, I yet know nothing in the arm of his friend from Missouri, either alone or when aided by the arm of his friend from South Carolina, that need deter even me from espousing whatever opinions I may choose to espouse, from debating whenever I may choose to debate, or from speaking whatever I may see fit to say on the floor of the Senate. Sir, when uttered as matter of commendation or compliment, I should dissent from nothing which the honorable member might say of his friend. Still less do I put forth any pretensions of my own. But when put to me as matter of taunt, I throw it back, and say to the gentleman that he could possibly say nothing less likely than such a comparison to wound my pride of persoꞩ ᵢᴸ character. The anger of its tone rescued the remark from intentional . irony, which, otherwise, probably, would have been its general accepta- tion. But, sir, if it be imagined that by this mutual quotation and com- mendation; if it be supposed that, by casting the characters of the drama, assigning to each his part, — to one the attack, to another the cry of onset, — or if it be thought that by a loud and empty vaunt of antici- pated victory any laurels are to be won here; if it be imagined, especially, that any or all these things will shake any purpose of mine, I can tell the honorable member, once for all, that he is greatly mistaken, and that he is dealing with one of whose temper and character he has yet much to learn. Sir, I shall not allow myself, on this occasion, — I hope on no occasion, — to be betrayed into any loss of temper; but if provoked, as I trust I never shall allow myself to be, into crimination and recrimination, the honorable member may, perhaps, find that in that contest there will be blows to take as well as blows to give; that others can state compari- sons as significant, at least, as his own; and that his impunity may, per- haps, demand of him whatever powers of taunt and sarcasm he may possess. I commend him to a prudent husbandry of his resources.

But, sir, the coalition! The coalition! Ay, "the murdered coalition"! The gentleman asks if I were led or frighted into this debate by the spectre of the coalition. — "Was it the ghost of the murdered coalition," he exclaims, "which haunted the member from Massachusetts, and which, like the ghost of Banquo, would never down?" "The murdered coali- tion!" Sir, this charge of a coalition, in reference to the late administra- tion, is not original with the honorable member. It did not spring up in the Senate. Whether as a fact, as an argument, or as an embellishment, it is all borrowed. He adopts it, indeed, from a very low origin, and a still lower present condition. It is one of the thousand calumnies with which the press teemed during an excited political canvass. It was a charge of which there was not only no proof or probability, but which was, in itself, wholly impossible to be true. No man of common infor- mation ever believed a syllable of it. Yet it was of that class of false- hoods which, by continued repetition through all the organs of detraction and abuse, are capable of misleading those who are already far misled, and of further fanning passion already kindling into flame. Doubtless it served its day, and, in a greater or less degree, the end designed by it. Having done that, it has sunk into the general mass of stale and loathed calumnies. It is the very cast-off slough of a polluted and shameless press. Incapable of further mischief, it lies in the sewer, lifeless and despised. It is not now, sir, in the power of the honorable member to give it dignity or decency, by attempting to elevate it, and to introduce it into the Senate. He cannot change it from what it is — an object of gen- eral disgust and scorn. On the contrary, the contact, if he choose to touch it, is more likely to drag him down, down, to the place where it lies itself.

But, sir, the honorable member was not, for other reasons, entirely happy in his allusion to the story of Banquo's murder and Banquo's ghost. It was not, I think, the friends, but the enemies of the murdered Banquo, at whose bidding his spirit would not down. The honorable gentleman is fresh in his reading of the English classics, and can put me right if I am wrong; but according to my poor recollection, it was at those who had begun with caresses, and ended with foul and treacherous murder, that the gory locks were shaken. The ghost of Banquo, like that of Hamlet, was an honest ghost. It disturbed no innocent man. It knew where its appearance would strike terror, and who would cry out, A ghost! It made itself visible in the right quarter, and compelled the guilty, and the conscience-smitten, and none others, to start, with

> " Prithee, see there! behold! — look! lo!
> If I stand here, I saw him! "

Their eyeballs were seared — was it not so, sir? — who had thought to shield themselves by concealing their own hand, and laying the imputation of the crime on a low and hireling agency in wickedness ; who had vainly attempted to stifle the workings of their own coward consciences, by ejaculating, through white lips and chattering teeth, " Thou canst not say I did it! " I have misread the great poet, if it was those who had no way partaken in the deed of the death, who either found that they were, *or feared that they should be*, pushed from their stools by the ghost of the slain, or who cried out to a spectre created by their own fears, and their own remorse, " Avaunt! and quit our sight! "

There is another particular, sir, in which the honorable member's quick perception of resemblances might, I should think, have seen something in the story of Banquo, making it not altogether a subject of the most pleasant contemplation. Those who murdered Banquo, what did they win by it? Substantial good? Permanent power? Or disappointment, rather, and sore mortification — dust and ashes — the common fate of vaulting ambition overleaping itself? Did not even-handed justice, ere long, commend the poisoned chalice to their own lips? Did they not soon find that for another they had " filed their mind "? — that their ambition, though apparently for the moment successful, had but put a barren sceptre in their grasp? Ay, sir, —

> " A barren sceptre in their gripe,
> *Thence to be wrenched by an unlineal hand,*
> *No son of theirs succeeding.*"

Sir, I need pursue the allusion no further. I leave the honorable gentleman to run it out at his leisure, and to derive from it all the gratification it is calculated to administer. If he finds himself pleased with the associations, and prepared to be quite satisfied, though the parallel should be entirely completed, I had almost said I am satisfied also — but that I shall think of. Yes, sir, I will think of that.

In the course of my observations the other day, Mr. President, I paid a passing tribute of respect to a very worthy man, Mr. Dane, of Massachusetts. It so happened, that he drew the ordinance of 1787 for the government of the North-western Territory. A man of so much ability, and so little pretence ; of so great a capacity to do good, and so unmixed a disposition to do it for its own sake ; a gentleman who acted an important part, forty years ago, in a measure the influence of which is still deeply felt in the very matter which was the subject of debate, might, I thought, receive from me a commendatory recognition.

But the honorable member was inclined to be facetious on the subject. He was rather disposed to make it matter of ridicule that I had introduced into the debate the name of one Nathan Dane, of whom he assures us he had never before heard. Sir, if the honorable member had never before heard of Mr. Dane, I am sorry for it. It shows him less acquainted with the public men of the country than I had supposed. Let me tell him, however, that a sneer from him at the mention of the name of Mr. Dane is in bad taste. It may well be a high mark of ambition, sir, either with the honorable gentleman or myself, to accomplish as much to make our names known to advantage, and remembered with gratitude, as Mr. Dane has accomplished. But the truth is, sir, I suspect that Mr. Dane lives a little too far north. He is of Massachusetts, and too near the north star to be reached by the honorable gentleman's telescope. If his sphere had happened to range south of Mason and Dixon's line, he might, probably, have come within the scope of his vision!

I spoke, sir, of the ordinance of 1787, which prohibited slavery in all future times north-west of the Ohio, as a measure of great wisdom and foresight, and one which had been attended with highly beneficial and permanent consequences. I supposed that on this point no two gentlemen in the Senate could entertain different opinions. But the simple expression of this sentiment has led the gentleman, not only into a labored defence of slavery in the abstract, and on principle, but also into a warm accusation against me, as having attacked the system of domestic slavery now existing in the Southern States. For all this there was not the slightest foundation in any thing said or intimated by me. I did not utter a single word which any ingenuity could torture into an attack on the slavery of the south. I said only that it was highly wise and useful in legislating for the north-western country, while it was yet a wilderness, to prohibit the introduction of slaves; and added, that I presumed, in the neighboring state of Kentucky, there was no reflecting and intelligent gentleman who would doubt that, if the same prohibition had been extended, at the same early period, over that commonwealth, her strength and population would, at this day, have been far greater than they are. If these opinions be thought doubtful, they are, nevertheless, I trust, neither extraordinary nor disrespectful. They attack nobody and menace nobody. And yet, sir, the gentleman's optics have discovered, even in the mere expression of this sentiment, what he calls the very spirit of the Missouri question! He represents me as making an onset on the whole south, and manifesting a spirit which would interfere with and disturb their domestic condition. Sir, this injustice no otherwise surprises me than as it is done here, and done without the slightest pretence of ground for it. I say it only surprises me as being done here; for I know full well that it is and has been the settled policy of some persons in the south, for years, to represent the people of the north as disposed to interfere with them in their own exclusive and peculiar concerns. This is a delicate and sensitive point in southern feeling; and of late years it has always been touched, and generally with effect, whenever the object has been to unite the whole south against northern men or northern measures. This feeling, always carefully kept alive, and maintained at too intense a heat to admit discrimination or reflection, is a lever of great power in our political machine. It moves vast bodies, and gives to them one and the same direction. But the feeling is without adequate cause, and the suspicion which exists wholly groundless. There is not, and never has been, a disposition in the north to interfere with these interests of the south Such interference has never been supposed to be within the power of government, nor has it been in any way attempted. It has always been regarded as a matter of domestic policy, left with the states themselves, and with which the federal government had nothing to do.

Certainly, sir, I am, and ever have been, of that opinion. The gentleman, indeed, argues that slavery in the abstract is no evil. Most assuredly I need not say I differ with him altogether and most widely on that point I regard domestic slavery as one of the greatest of evils, both moral and political. But, though it be a malady, and whether it be curable, and if so, by what means; or, on the other hand, whether it be the *vulnus immedicabile* of the social system, I leave it to those whose right and duty it is to inquire and to decide. And this I believe, sir, is, and uniformly has been, the sentiment of the north. Let us look a little at the history of this matter.

When the present constitution was submitted for the ratification of the people, there were those who imagined that the powers of the government which it proposed to establish might, perhaps, in some possible mode, be exerted in measures tending to the abolition of slavery. This suggestion would, of course, attract much attention in the southern conventions. In that of Virginia, Governor Randolph said, —

"I hope there is none here, who, considering the subject in the calm light of philosophy, will make an objection dishonorable to Virginia — that, at the moment they are securing the rights of their citizens, an objection is started, that there is a spark of hope that those unfortunate men now held in bondage may, by the operation of the general government, be made free."

At the very first Congress petitions on the subject were presented, if I mistake not, from different states. The Pennsylvania Society for promoting the Abolition of Slavery took a lead, and laid before Congress a memorial, praying Congress to promote the abolition by such powers as it possessed. This memorial was referred, in the House of Representatives, to a select committee, consisting of Mr. Foster, of New Hampshire, Mr. Gerry, of Massachusetts, Mr. Huntington, of Connecticut, Mr. Lawrence, of New York, Mr. Sinnickson, of New Jersey, Mr. Hartley, of Pennsylvania, and Mr. Parker, of Virginia; all of them, sir, as you will observe, northern men, but the last. This committee made a report, which was committed to a committee of the whole house, and there considered and discussed on several days; and being amended, although in no material respect, it was made to express three distinct propositions on the subjects of slavery and the slave trade. First, in the words of the constitution, that Congress could not, prior to the year 1808, prohibit the migration or importation of such persons as any of the states then existing should think proper to admit. Second, that Congress had authority to restrain the citizens of the United States from carrying on the African slave trade for the purpose of supplying foreign countries. On this proposition, our early laws against those who engage in that traffic are founded The third proposition, and that which bears on the present question, was expressed in the following terms : —

"*Resolved*, That Congress have no authority to interfere in the emancipation of slaves, or in the treatment of them in any of the states; it remaining with the several states alone to provide rules and regulations therein, which humanity and true policy may require."

This resolution received the sanction of the House of Representatives so early as March, 1790. And, now, sir, the honorable member will allow me to remind him, that not only were the select committee who reported the resolution, with a single exception, all northern men, but also that of the members then composing the House of Representatives, a large majority, I believe nearly two thirds, were northern men also.

The house agreed to insert these resolutions in its journal; and, from that day to this, it has never been maintained or contended that Congress had any authority to regulate or interfere with the condition of slaves in the several states. No northern gentleman, to my knowledge, has moved any such question in either house of Congress.

The fears of the south, whatever fears they might have entertained, were allayed and quieted by this early decision; and so remained, till they were excited afresh, without cause, but for collateral and indirect purposes. When it became necessary, or was thought so, by some political persons, to find an unvarying ground for the exclusion of northern men from confidence and from lead in the affairs of the republic, then, and not till then, the cry was raised, and the feeling industriously excited, that the influence of northern men in the public councils would endanger the relation of master and slave. For myself, I claim no other merit, than that this gross and enormous injustice towards the whole north has not wrought upon me to change my opinions, or my political conduct. I hope I am above violating my principles, even under the smart of injury and false imputations. Unjust suspicions and undeserved reproach, whatever pain I may experience from them, will not induce me, I trust, nevertheless, to overstep the limits of constitutional duty, or to encroach on the rights of others. The domestic slavery of the south I leave where I find it — in the hands of their own governments. It is their affair, not mine. Nor do I complain of the peculiar effect which the magnitude of that population has had in the distribution of power under this federal government. We know, sir, that the representation of the states in the other house is not equal. We know that great advantage, in that respect, is enjoyed by the slaveholding states; and we know, too, that the intended equivalent for that advantage — that is to say, the imposition of direct taxes in the same ratio — has become merely nominal; the habit of the government being almost invariably to collect its revenues from other sources, and in other modes. Nevertheless, I do not complain; nor would I countenance any movement to alter this arrangement of representation. It is the original bargain, the compact — let it stand; let the advantage of it be fully enjoyed. The Union itself is too full of benefit to be hazarded in propositions for changing its original basis. I go for the constitution as it is, and for the Union as it is. But I am resolved not to submit, in silence, to accusations, either against myself individually, or against the north, wholly unfounded and unjust — accusations which impute to us a disposition to evade the constitutional compact, and to extend the power of the government over the internal laws and domestic condition of the states. All such accusations, wherever and whenever made, all insinuations of the existence of any such purposes, I know and feel to be groundless and injurious. And we must confide in southern gentlemen themselves; we must trust to those whose integrity of heart and magnanimity of feeling will lead them to a desire to maintain and disseminate truth, and who possess the means of its diffusion with the southern public; we must leave it to them to disabuse that public of its prejudices. But, in the mean time, for my own part, I shall continue to act justly, whether those towards whom justice is exercised receive it with candor or with contumely.

Having had occasion to recur to the ordinance of 1787, in order to defend myself against the inferences which the honorable member has chosen to draw from my former observations on that subject, I am not willing now entirely to take leave of it without another remark. It need hardly be said, that that paper expresses just sentiments on the great subject of civil and religious liberty. Such sentiments were common, and abound in all our state papers of that day. But this ordinance did that which was not so common, and which is not, even now, universal; that is, it set forth and declared, *as a high and binding duty of government itself*, to encourage schools and advance the means of education; on the plain reason that religion, morality, and knowledge are necessary to good government, and to the happiness of mankind. One observation further. The important provision incorporated into the constitution of the United States, and several of those of the states, and recently, as we have seen, adopted into the reformed constitution of Virginia, restraining legislative power, in questions of private right, and from impairing the obligation of contracts, is first introduced and established, as far as I am informed, as matter of express written constitutional law, in this ordinance of 1787. And I must add, also, in regard to the author of the ordinance, who has not had the happiness to attract the gentleman's notice heretofore, nor to avoid his sarcasm now, that he was chairman of that select committee of the old Congress, whose report first expressed the strong sense of that body, that the old confederation was not adequate to the exigencies of the country, and recommending to the states to send delegates to the convention which formed the present constitution.

An attempt has been made to transfer from the north to the south the honor of this exclusion of slavery from the North-western Territory. The journal, without argument or comment, refutes such attempt. The session of Virginia was made March, 1784. On the 19th of April following, a committee, consisting of Messrs. Jefferson, Chase, and Howell, reported a plan for a temporary government of the territory, in which was this article : " That after the year 1800, there shall be neither slavery nor involuntary servitude, in any of the said states, otherwise than in punishment of crimes, whereof the party shall have been convicted." Mr. Speight, of North Carolina, moved to strike out this paragraph. The question was put, according to the form then practised : " Shall these words stand, as part of the plan," &c. New Hampshire, Massachusetts, Rhode Island, Connecticut, New York, New Jersey, and Pennsylvania — seven states — voted in the affirmative; Maryland, Virginia, and South Carolina in the negative. North Carolina was divided. As the consent of nine states was necessary, the words could not stand, and were struck out accordingly. Mr. Jefferson voted for the clause, but was overruled by his colleagues.

In March of the next year, (1785,) Mr. King, of Massachusetts, seconded by Mr. Ellery, of Rhode Island, proposed the formerly rejected article, with this addition : " *And that this regulation shall be an article of compact, and remain a fundamental principle of the constitution between the thirteen original states and each of the states described in the resolve*," &c. On this clause, which provided the adequate and thorough security, the eight Northern States, at that time, voted affirmatively, and the four Southern States negatively. The votes of nine states were not yet obtained, and thus the provision was again rejected by the Southern States. The perseverance of the north held out, and two years afterwards the object was attained. It is no derogation from the credit, whatever that may be, of drawing the ordinance, that its principles had before been prepared and discussed, in the form of resolutions. If one should reason in that way, what would become of the distinguished honor of the author of the Declaration of Independence? There is not a sentiment in that paper which had not been voted and resolved in the assemblies, and other popular bodies in the country, over and over again.

But the honorable member has now found out that this gentleman, Mr. Dane, was a member of the Hartford Convention. However uninformed the honorable member may be of characters and occurrences at the north, it would seem that he has at his elbows, on this occasion, some high-minded and lofty spirit, some magnanimous and true-hearted monitor, possessing the means of local knowledge, and ready to supply the honorable member with every thing, down even to forgotten and moth-eaten twopenny pamphlets, which may be used to the disadvantage of his own country. But, as to the Hartford Convention, sir, allow me to say, that the proceedings of that body seem now to be less read and studied in New England than farther south. They appear to be looked to, not in New England, but elsewhere, for the purpose of seeing how far they may serve as a precedent. But they will not answer the purpose — they are quite too tame. The latitude in which they originated was too cold. Other conventions, of more recent existence, have gone a whole bar's length beyond it. The learned doctors of Colleton and Abbeville have pushed their commentaries on the Hartford collect so far that the original text writers are thrown entirely into the shade. I have nothing to do, sir, with the Hartford Convention. Its journal, which the gentleman has quoted, I never read. So far as the honorable member may discover in its proceedings a spirit in any degree resembling that which was avowed and justified in those other conventions to which I have alluded, or so far as those proceedings can be shown to be disloyal to the constitution, or tending to disunion, so far I shall be as ready as any one to bestow on them reprehension and censure.

Having dwelt long on this convention, and other occurrences of that day, in the hope, probably, (which will not be gratified,) that I should leave the course of this debate to follow him at length in those excursions, the honorable member returned, and attempted another object. He referred to a speech of mine in the other house, the same which I had occasion to allude to myself the other day; and has quoted a passage or two from it, with a bold though uneasy and laboring air of confidence, as if he had detected in me an inconsistency. Judging from the gentleman's manner, a stranger to the course of the debate, and to the point in discussion, would have imagined, from so triumphant a tone, that the honorable member was about to overwhelm me with a manifest contradiction. Any one who heard him, and who had not heard what I had, in fact, previously said, must have thought me routed and discomfited, as the gentleman had promised. Sir, a breath blows all this triumph away. There is not the slightest difference in the sentiments of my remarks on the two occasions. What I said here on Wednesday is in exact accordance with the opinions expressed by me in the other house in 1825. Though the gentleman had the metaphysics of Hudibras — though he were able

" to sever and divide
A hair 'twixt north and north-west side,"

he could not yet insert his metaphysical scissors between the fair reading of my remarks in 1825 and what I said here last week. There is not only no contradiction, no difference, but, in truth, too exact a similarity, both in thought and language, to be entirely in just taste. I had myself quoted the same speech; had recurred to it, and spoke with it open before me; and much of what I said was little more than a repetition from it. In order to make finishing work with this alleged contradiction, permit me to recur to the origin of this debate, and review its course. This seems expedient, and may be done as well now as at any time.

Well, then, its history is this: The honorable member from Connecticut moved a resolution, which constituted the first branch of that which is now before us; that is to say, a resolution instructing the committee on public lands to inquire into the expediency of limiting, for a certain period, the sales of public lands to such as have heretofore been offered for sale; and whether sundry offices, connected with the sales of the lands, might not be abolished without detriment to the public service.

In the progress of the discussion which arose on this resolution, an honorable member from New Hampshire moved to amend the resolution, so as entirely to reverse its object; that is, to strike it all out, and insert a direction to the committee to inquire into the expediency of adopting measures to hasten the sales, and extend more rapidly the surveys of the lands.

The honorable member from Maine (Mr. Sprague) suggested that both these propositions might well enough go, for consideration, to the committee; and in this state of the question, the member from South Carolina addressed the Senate in his first speech. He rose, he said, to give us his own free thoughts on the public lands. I saw him rise, with pleasure, and listened with expectation, though before he concluded I was filled with surprise. Certainly, I was never more surprised than to find him following up, to the extent he did, the sentiments and opinions which the gentleman from Missouri had put forth, and which it is known he has long entertained.

I need not repeat, at large, the general topics of the honorable gentleman's speech. When he said, yesterday, that he did not attack the Eastern States, he certainly must have forgotten not only particular remarks, but the whole drift and tenor of his speech; unless he means by not attacking, that he did not commence hostilities, but that another had preceded him in the attack. He, in the first place, disapproved of the whole course of the government for forty years, in regard to its dispositions of the public land; and then, turning northward and eastward, and fancying he had found a cause for alleged narrowness and niggardliness in the "accursed policy" of the tariff, to which he represented the people of New England as wedded, he went on, for a full hour, with remarks, the whole scope of which was to exhibit the results of this policy, in feelings and in measures unfavorable to the west. I thought his opinions unfounded and erroneous, as to the general course of the government, and ventured to reply to them.

The gentleman had remarked on the analogy of other cases, and quoted the conduct of European governments towards their own subjects, settling on this continent, as in point, to show that we had been harsh and rigid in selling when we should have given the public lands to settlers. I thought the honorable member had suffered his judgment to be betrayed by a false analogy; that he was struck with an appearance of

4

resemblance where there was no real similitude. I think so still. The first settlers of North America were enterprising spirits, engaged in private adventure, or fleeing from tyranny at home. When arrived here, they were forgotten by the mother country, or remembered only to be oppressed. Carried away again by the appearance of analogy, or struck with the eloquence of the passage, the honorable member yesterday observed that the conduct of government towards the western emigrants, or my representation of it, brought to his mind a celebrated speech in the British Parliament. It was, sir, the speech of Colonel Barré. On the question of the stamp act, or tea tax, I forget which, Colonel Barré had heard a member on the treasury bench argue, that the people of the United States, being British colonists, planted by the maternal care, nourished by the indulgence, and protected by the arms of England, would not grudge their mite to relieve the mother country from the heavy burden under which she groaned. The language of Colonel Barré, in reply to this, was, " They planted by your care? Your oppression planted them in America. They fled from your tyranny, and grew by your neglect of them. So soon as you began to care for them, you showed your care by sending persons to spy out their liberties, misrepresent their character, prey upon them, and eat out their substance."

And now does the honorable gentleman mean to maintain that language like this is applicable to the conduct of the government of the United States towards the western emigrants, or to any representation given by me of that conduct? Were the settlers in the west driven thither by our oppression? Have they flourished only by our neglect of them? Has the government done nothing but to prey upon them, and eat out their substance? Sir, this fervid eloquence of the British speaker, just when and where it was uttered, and fit to remain an exercise for the schools, is not a little out of place, when it was brought thence to be applied here, to the conduct of our own country towards her own citizens. From America to England it may be true; from Americans to their own government it would be strange language. Let us leave it to be recited and declaimed by our boys against a foreign nation; not introduce it here, to recite and declaim ourselves against our own.

But I come to the point of the alleged contradiction. In my remarks on Wednesday, I contended that we could not give away gratuitously all the public lands; that we held them in trust; that the government had solemnly pledged itself to dispose of them as a common fund for the common benefit, and to sell and settle them as its discretion should dictate. Now, sir, what contradiction does the gentleman find to this sentiment in the speech of 1825? He quotes me as having then said, that we ought not to hug these lands as a very great treasure. Very well, sir; supposing me to be accurately reported in that expression, what is the contradiction? I have not now said, that we should hug these lands as a favorite source of pecuniary income. No such thing. It is not my view. What I have said, and what I do say, is, that they are a common fund — to be disposed of for the common benefit — to be sold at low prices, for the accommodation of settlers, keeping the object of settling the lands as much in view as that of raising money from them. This I say now, and this I have always said. Is this hugging them as a favorite treasure? Is there no difference between hugging and hoarding this fund, on the one hand, as a great treasure, and on the other of disposing of it at low prices, placing the proceeds in the general treasury of the Union? My opinion is, that as much is to be made of the land, as fairly and reasonably **may** be, selling it all the while at such rates as to give the fullest effect to settlement. This is not giving it all away to the states, as the gentleman would propose; nor is it hugging the fund closely and tenaciously, as a favorite treasure; but it is, in my judgment, a just and wise policy, perfectly according with all the various duties which rest on government. So much for my contradiction. And what is it? Where is the ground of the gentleman's triumph? What inconsistency, in word or doctrine, has he been able to detect? Sir, if this be a sample of that discomfiture with which the honorable gentleman threatened me, commend me to the word *discomfiture* for the rest of my life.

But, after all, this is not the point of the debate; and I must bring the gentleman back to that which is the point.

The real question between me and him is, Where has the doctrine been advanced, at the south or the east, that the population of the west should be retarded, or, at least, need not be hastened, on account of its effect to drain off the people from the Atlantic States? Is this doctrine, as has been alleged, of eastern origin? That is the question. Has the gentleman found any thing by which he can make good his accusation? I submit to the Senate, that he has entirely failed; and as far as this debate has shown, the only person who has advanced such sentiments is a gentleman from South Carolina, and a friend to the honorable member himself. The honorable gentleman has given no answer to this; there is none which can be given. This simple fact, while it requires no comment to enforce it, defies all argument to refute it. I could refer to the speeches of another southern gentleman, in years before, of the same general character, and to the same effect, as that which has been quoted; but I will not consume the time of the Senate by the reading of them.

So then, sir, New England is guiltless of the policy of retarding western population, and of all envy and jealousy of the growth of the new states. Whatever there be of that policy in the country, no part of it is hers. If it has a local habitation, the honorable member has probably seen, by this time, where he is to look for it; and if it now has received a name, he himself has christened it.

We approach, at length, sir, to a more important part of the honorable gentleman's observations. Since it does not accord with my views of justice and policy to vote away the public lands altogether, as mere matter of gratuity, I am asked, by the honorable gentleman, on what ground it is that I consent to give them away in particular instances. How, he inquires, do I reconcile with these professed sentiments my support of measures appropriating portions of the lands to particular roads, particular canals, particular rivers, and particular institutions of education in the west? This leads, sir, to the real and wide difference in political opinions between the honorable gentleman and myself. On my part, I look upon all these objects as connected with the common good, fairly embraced in its objects and its terms; he, on the contrary, deems them all, if good at all, only local good. This is our difference. The interrogatory which he proceeded to put at once explains this difference. "What interest," asks he, "has South Carolina in a canal in Ohio?" Sir, this very question is full of significance. It develops the gentleman's whole political system; and its answer expounds mine. Here we differ *toto cœlo*. I look upon a road over the Alleghany, a canal round the falls of the Ohio, or a canal or railway from the Atlantic to the western waters, as being objects large and extensive enough to be fairly said to be for the common benefit. The gentleman thinks otherwise, and this is the key to open his construction of the powers of the government. He may well ask, upon his system, What interest has South Carolina in a canal in Ohio? On that system, it is true, she has no interest. On that system, Ohio and Carolina are different governments and different countries, connected here, it is true, by some slight and ill-defined bond of union, but in all main respects separate and diverse On that system, Carolina has no more interest in a canal in Ohio than in Mexico. The gentleman, therefore, only follows out his own principles; he does no more than arrive at the natural conclusions of his own doctrines; he only announces the true results of that creed which he has adopted himself, and would persuade others to adopt, when he thus declares that South Carolina has no interest in a public work in Ohio. Sir, we narrow-minded people of New England do not reason thus. Our notion of things is entirely different. We look upon the states, not as separated, but as united. We love to dwell on that Union, and on the mutual happiness which it has so much promoted, and the common renown which it has so greatly contributed to acquire. In our contemplation, Carolina and Ohio are parts of the same country — states united under the same general government, having interests common, associated, intermingled. In whatever is within the proper sphere of the constitutional power of this government, we look upon the states as one. We do not impose geographical limits to our patriotic feeling or regard; we do not follow rivers, and mountains, and lines of latitude, to find boundaries beyond which public improvements do not benefit us. We, who come here as agents and representatives of those narrow-minded and selfish men of New England, consider ourselves as bound to regard, with equal eye, the good of the whole, in whatever is within our power of legislation. Sir, if a railroad or a canal, beginning in South Carolina, and ending in South Carolina, appeared to me to be of national importance and national magnitude, believing as I do that the power of government extends to the encouragement of works of that description, if I were to stand up here and ask, " What interest has Massachusetts in a railroad in South Carolina?" I should not be willing to face my constituents. These same narrow-minded men would tell me that they had sent me to act for the whole country, and that one who possessed too little comprehension, either of intellect or feeling, — one who was not large enough, in mind and heart, to embrace the whole, — was not fit to be intrusted with the interest of any part. Sir, I do not desire to enlarge the powers of the government by unjustifiable construction, nor to exercise any not within a fair interpretation. But when it is believed that a power does exist, then it is, in my judgment, to be exercised for the general benefit of the whole : so far as respects the exercise of such a power, the states are one. It was the very object of the constitution to create unity of interests to the extent of the powers of the general government. In war and peace we are one; in commerce one; because the authority of the general government reaches to war and peace, and to the regulation of commerce. I have never seen any more difficulty in erecting lighthouses on the lakes than on the ocean in improving the harbors of inland seas, than if they were within the ebb and flow of the tide; or of removing obstructions in the vast streams of the west, more than in any work to facilitate commerce on the Atlantic coast. If there be power for one, there is power also for the other; and they are all and equally for the country.

There are other objects, apparently more local, or the benefit of which is less general, towards which, nevertheless, I have concurred with others to give aid by donations of land. It is proposed to construct a road in or through one of the new states in which this government possesses large quantities of land. Have the United States no right, as a great and untaxed proprietor — are they under no obligation — to contribute to an object thus calculated to promote the common good of all the proprietors, themselves included? And even with respect to education, which is the extreme case, let the question be considered. In the first place, as we have seen, it was made matter of compact with these states they they should do their part to promote education. In the next place, our whole system of land laws proceeds on the idea that education is for the common good; because, in every division, a certain portion is uniformly reserved and appropriated for the use of schools. And, finally, have not these new states singularly strong claims, founded on the ground already stated, that the government is a great untaxed proprietor in the ownership of the soil? It is a consideration of great importance that probably there is in no part of the country, or of the world, so great a call for the means of education as in those new states, owing to the vast number of persons within those ages in which education and instruction are usually received, if received at all. This is the natural consequence of recency of settlement and rapid increase. The census of these states shows how great a proportion of the whole population occupies the classes between infancy and manhood. These are the wide fields, and here is the deep and quick soil for the seeds of knowledge and virtue; and this is the favored season, the spring time for sowing them. Let them be disseminated without stint. Let them be scattered with a bountiful broadcast. Whatever the government can fairly do towards these objects, in my opinion, ought to be done.

These, sir, are the grounds, succinctly stated, on which my votes for grants of lands for particular objects rest, while I maintain, at the same time, that it is all a common fund, for the common benefit. And reasons like these, I presume, have influenced the votes of other gentlemen from New England. Those who have a different view of the powers of the government, of course, come to different conclusions on these as on other questions. I observed, when speaking on this subject before, that if we looked to any measure, whether for a road, a canal, or any thing else intended for the improvement of the west, it would be found, that if the New England ayes were struck out of the list of votes, the southern noes would always have rejected the measure. The truth of this has not been denied, and cannot be denied. In stating this, I thought it just to ascribe it to the constitutional scruples of the south, rather than to any other less favorable or less charitable cause. But no sooner had I done this, than the honorable gentleman asks if I reproach him and his friends with their constitutional scruples. Sir, I reproach nobody. I stated a fact, and gave the most respectful reason for it that occurred to me. The gentleman cannot deny the fact — he may, if he choose, disclaim the reason. It is not long since I had occasion, in presenting a petition from his own state, to account for its being intrusted to my hands by saying, that the constitutional opinions of the gentleman and his worthy colleague prevented them from supporting it. Sir, did I state this as a matter of reproach? Far from it. Did I attempt to find any other cause than an honest one for these scruples? Sir, I did not. It did not become me to doubt, nor to insinuate that the gentleman had either changed his sentiments, or that he had made up a set of constitutional opinions, accommodated to any particular combination of political occurrences. Had I done so, I should have felt, that while I was entitled to little respect in thus questioning other people's motives, I justified the whole world in suspecting my own.

But how has the gentleman returned this respect for others' opinions? His own candor and justice, how have they been exhibited towards the motives of others, while he has been at so much pains to maintain — what nobody has disputed — the purity of his own? Why, sir, he has asked *when*, and *how*, and *why* New England votes were found going for measures favorable to the west; he has demanded to be informed whether all this did not begin in 1825, *and while the election of president was still pending*. Sir, to these questions retort would be justified; and it is both cogent and at hand. Nevertheless, I will answer the inquiry not by retort, but by facts. I will tell the gentleman *when*, and *how*, and *why* New England has supported measures favorable to the west. I have already referred to the early history of the government — to the first acquisition of the lands — to the original laws for disposing of them and for governing the territories where they lie; and have shown the influence of New England men and New England principles in all these leading measures. I should not be pardoned were I to go over that ground again. Coming to more recent times, and to measures of a less general character, I have endeavored to prove that every thing of this kind designed for western improvement has depended on the votes of New England. All this is true beyond the power of contradiction.

And now, sir, there are two measures to which I will refer, not so ancient as to belong to the early history of the public lands, and not so recent as to be on this side of the period when the gentleman charitably imagines a new direction may have been given to New England feeling and New England votes. These measures, and the New England votes in support of them, may be taken as samples and specimens of all the rest. In 1820, (observe, Mr. President, in 1820,) the people of the west besought Congress for a reduction in the price of lands. In favor of that reduction, New England, with a delegation of forty members in the other house, gave thirty-three votes, and one only against it. The four Southern States, with fifty members, gave thirty-two votes for it, and seven against it. Again, in 1821, (observe again, sir, the time,) the law passed for the relief of the purchasers of the public lands. This was a measure of vital importance to the west, and more especially to the south-west. It authorized the relinquishment of contracts for lands, which had been entered into at high prices, and a reduction, in other cases, of not less than 37½ per cent. on the purchase money. Many millions of dollars, six or seven I believe, at least, — probably much more, — were relinquished by this law. On this bill New England, with her forty members, gave more affirmative votes than the four Southern States with their fifty-two or three members. These two are far the most important measures respecting the public lands which have been adopted within the last twenty years. They took place in 1820 and 1821. That is the time when. And as to the manner how, the gentleman already sees that it was by voting, in solid column, for the required relief; and lastly, as to the cause why, I tell the gentleman, it was because the members from New England thought the measures just and salutary; because they entertained towards the west neither envy, hatred, nor malice; because they deemed it becoming them, as just and enlightened public men, to meet the exigency which had arisen in the west with the appropriate measure of relief; because they felt it due to their own characters, and the characters of their New England predecessors in this government, to act towards the new states in the spirit of a liberal, patronizing, magnanimous policy. So much, sir, for the cause *why;* and I hope that by this time, sir, the honorable gentleman is satisfied; if not, I do not know *when*, or *how*, or *why*, he ever will be.

Having recurred to these two important measures, in answer to the gentleman's inquiries, I must now beg permission to go back to a period still something earlier, for the purpose still further of showing how much, or rather how little, reason there is for the gentleman's insinuation that political hopes, or fears, or party associations, were the grounds of these New England votes. And after what has been said, I hope it may be forgiven me if I allude to some political opinions and votes of my own, of very little public importance, certainly, but which, from the time at which they were given and expressed, may pass for good witnesses on this occasion.

This government, Mr. President, from its origin to the peace of 1815, had been too much engrossed with various other important concerns to be able to turn its thoughts inward, and look to the development of its vast internal resources. In the early part of President Washington's administration, it was fully occupied with organizing the government, providing for the public debt, defending the frontiers, and maintaining domestic peace. Before the termination of that administration, the fires of the French revolution blazed forth, as from a new-opened volcano, and the whole breadth of the ocean did not entirely secure us from its effects. The smoke and the cinders reached us, though not the burning lava. Difficult and agitating questions, embarrassing to government, and dividing public opinion, sprung out of the new state of our foreign relations, and were succeeded by others, and yet again by others, equally embarrassing, and equally exciting division and discord, through the long series of twenty years, till they finally issued in the war with England. Down to the close of that war, no distinct, marked, and deliberate attention had been given, or could have been given, to the internal condition of the country, its capacities of improvement, or the constitutional power of the government, in regard to objects connected with such improvement.

The peace, Mr. President, brought about an entirely new and a most interesting state of things; it opened to us other prospects, and suggested other duties; we ourselves were changed, and the whole world was changed. The pacification of Europe, after June, 1815, assumed a firm and permanent aspect. The nations evidently manifested that they were disposed for peace: some agitation of the waves might be expected, even after the storm had subsided; but the tendency was, strongly and rapidly, towards settled repose.

It so happened, sir, that I was at that time a member of Congress, and, like others, naturally turned my attention to the contemplation of the newly-altered condition of the country, and of the world. It appeared plainly enough to me, as well as to wiser and more experienced men, that the policy of the government would necessarily take a start in a new direction ; because new directions would necessarily be given to the pursuits and occupations of the people.   We had pushed our commerce far and fast, under the advantage of a neutral flag.   But there were now no longer flags, either neutral or belligerent.   The harvest of neutrality had been great, but we had gathered it all.   With the peace of Europe, it was obvious there would spring up, in her circle of nations, a revived and invigorated spirit of trade, and a new activity in all the business and objects of civilized life.   Hereafter, our commercial gains were to be earned only by success in a close and intense competition.   Other nations would produce for themselves, and carry for themselves, and manufacture for themselves, to the full extent of their abilities.   The crops of our plains would no longer sustain European armies, nor our ships longer supply those whom war had rendered unable to supply themselves.   It was obvious, that, under these circumstances, the country would begin to survey itself, and to estimate its own capacity of improvement.   And this improvement, how was it to be accomplished, and who was to accomplish it ?

We were ten or twelve millions of people, spread over almost half a world.   We were twenty-four states, some stretching along the same seaboard, some along the same line of inland frontier, and others on opposite banks of the same vast rivers.   Two considerations at once presented themselves, in looking at this state of things, with great force.   One was, that that great branch of improvement, which consisted in furnishing new facilities of intercourse, necessarily ran into different states, in every leading instance, and would benefit the citizens of all such states.   No one state, therefore, in such cases, would assume the whole expense, nor was the cooperation of several states to be expected.   Take the instance of the Delaware Breakwater.   It will cost several millions of money.   Would Pennsylvania alone have ever constructed it ?   Certainly never, while this Union lasts, because it is not for her sole benefit.   Would Pennsylvania, New Jersey, and Delaware have united to accomplish it, at their joint expense?   Certainly not, for the same reason.   It could not be done, therefore, but by the general government.   The same may be said of the large inland undertakings, except that, in them, government, instead of bearing the whole expense, cooperates with others who bear a part.   The other consideration is, that the United States have the means.   They enjoy the revenues derived from commerce, and the states have no abundant and easy sources of public income.   The custom houses fill the general treasury, while the states have scanty resources, except by resort to heavy direct taxes.

Under this view of things, I thought it necessary to settle, at least for myself, some definite notions, with respect to the powers of government, in regard to internal affairs.   It may not savor too much of self-commendation to remark, that, with this object, I considered the constitution, its judicial construction, its contemporaneous exposition, and the whole history of the legislation of Congress under it; and I arrived at the conclusion that government has power to accomplish sundry objects, or aid in their accomplishment, which are now commonly spoken of as INTERNAL IMPROVEMENTS.   That conclusion, sir, may have been right, or it may have been wrong.   I am not about to argue the grounds of it at large.   I say only that it was adopted, and acted on, even so early as in 1816.   Yes, Mr. President, I made up my opinion, and determined on my intended course of political conduct on these subjects, in the 14th Congress, in 1816. And now, Mr. President, I have further to say, that I made up these opinions, and entered on this course of political conduct, *Teucro duce.* Yes, sir, I pursued, in all this, a South Carolina track. On the doctrines of internal improvement, South Carolina, as she was then represented in the other house, set forth, in 1816, under a fresh and leading breeze; and I was among the followers. But if my leader sees new lights, and turns a sharp corner, unless I see new lights also, I keep straight on in the same path. I repeat, that leading gentlemen from South Carolina were first and foremost in behalf of the doctrines of internal improvements, when those doctrines first came to be considered and acted upon in Congress. The debate on the bank question, on the tariff of 1816, and on the direct tax, will show who was who, and what was what, at that time. The tariff of 1816, one of the plain cases of oppression and usurpation, from which, if the government does not recede, individual states may justly secede from the government, is, sir, in truth, a South Carolina tariff, supported by South Carolina votes. But for those votes, it could not have passed in the form in which it did pass; whereas, if it had depended on Massachusetts votes, it would have been lost. Does not the honorable gentleman well know all this? There are certainly those who do full well know it all. I do not say this to reproach South Carolina; I only state the fact, and I think it will appear to be true, that among the earliest and boldest advocates of the tariff, as a measure of protection, and on the express ground of protection, were leading gentlemen of South Carolina in Congress. I did not then, and cannot now, understand their language in any other sense. While this tariff of 1816 was under discussion in the House of Representatives, an honorable gentleman from Georgia, now of this house, (Mr. Forsyth,) moved to reduce the proposed duty on cotton. He failed by four votes, South Carolina giving three votes (enough to have turned the scale) against his motion. The act, sir, then passed, and received on its passage the support of a majority of the representatives of South Carolina present and voting. This act is the first, in the order of those now denounced as plain usurpations. We see it daily in the list by the side of those of 1824 and 1828, as a case of manifest oppression, justifying disunion. I put it home to the honorable member from South Carolina, that his own state was not only "art and part" in this measure, but the *causa causans.* Without her aid, this seminal principle of mischief, this root of upas, could not have been planted. I have already said — and it is true — that this act proceeded on the ground of protection. It interfered directly with existing interests of great value and amount. It cut up the Calcutta cotton trade by the roots. But it passed, nevertheless, and it passed on the principle of protecting manufactures, on the principle against free trade, on the principle *opposed to that which lets us alone.*

Such, Mr. President, were the opinions of important and leading gentlemen of South Carolina, on the subject of internal improvement, in 1816. I went out of Congress the next year, and returning again in 1823, thought I found South Carolina where I had left her. I really supposed that all things remained as they were, and that the South Carolina doctrine of internal improvements would be defended by the same eloquent voices and the same strong arms, as formerly. In the lapse of these six year , it is true, political associations had assumed a new aspect and new div ns. A party had arisen in the south, hostile to the doctrine of internal improvements, and had vigorously attacked that doctrine. Anti-consolidation was the flag under which this party fought, and its supporters inveighed against internal improvements, much after the same manner in which the honorable gentleman has now inveighed against them, as part and parcel of the system of consolidation.

Whether this party arose in South Carolina herself, or in her neighborhood, is more than I know. I think the latter. However that may have been, there were those found in South Carolina ready to make war upon it, and who did make intrepid war upon it. Names being regarded as things, in such controversies, they bestowed on the anti-improvement gentlemen the appellation of radicals. Yes, sir, the name of radicals, as a term of distinction, applicable and applied to those who denied the liberal doctrines of internal improvements, originated, according to the best of my recollection, somewhere between North Carolina and Georgia. Well, sir, those mischievous radicals were to be put down, and the strong arm of South Carolina was stretched out to put them down. About this time, sir, I returned to Congress. The battle with the radicals had been fought, and our South Carolina champions of the doctrines of internal improvement had nobly maintained their ground, and were understood to have achieved a victory. They had driven back the enemy with discomfiture ; a thing, by the way, sir, which is not always performed when it is promised. A gentleman, to whom I have already referred in this debate, had come into Congress, during my absence from it, from South Carolina, and had brought with him a high reputation for ability. He came from a school with which we had been acquainted, *et noscitur a sociis*. I hold in my hand, sir, a printed speech of this distinguished gentleman, (Mr. McDuffie,) " on internal improvements," delivered about the period to which I now refer, and printed with a few introductory remarks upon consolidation ; in which, sir, I think he quite consolidated the arguments of his opponents, the radicals, if to *crush* be to consolidate. I give you a short but substantive quotation from these remarks. He is speaking of a pamphlet, then recently published, entitled " Consolidation ; " and having alluded to the question of rechartering the former Bank of the United States, he says, " Moreover, in the early history of parties, and when Mr. Crawford advocated the renewal of the old charter, it was considered a federal measure ; which internal improvement never was, as this author erroneously states. This latter measure originated in the administration of Mr. Jefferson, with the appropriation for the Cumberland road ; and was first proposed, *as a system*, by Mr. Calhoun, and carried through the House of Representatives by a large majority of the republicans, including almost every one of the leading men who carried us through the late war."

So then, internal improvement is not one of the federal heresies.

One paragraph more, sir.

" The author in question, not content with denouncing as federalists General Jackson, Mr. Adams, Mr. Calhoun, and the majority of the South Carolina delegation in Congress, modestly extends the denunciation to Mr. Monroe and the whole republican party. Here are his words : ' During the administration of Mr. Monroe, much has passed which the republican party would be glad to approve, if they could ! ! But the principal feature, and that which has chiefly elicited these observations, is the renewal of the system of internal improveme⌐ s.' Now, this measure was adopted by a vote of 115 to 86, of a repu⌐ can Congress, and sanctioned by a republican president. Who, then, is this author, who assumes the high prerogative of denouncing, in the name of the republican party, the republican administration of the country — a denunciation including within its sweep Calhoun, Lowndes, and Cheves; men who will be regarded as the brightest ornaments of South Carolina, and the strongest pillars of the republican party, as long as the late war shall be remembered, and talents and patriotism shall be regarded as the proper objects of the admiration and gratitude of a free people!!"

Such are the opinions, sir, which were maintained by South Carolina gentlemen in the House of Representatives on the subject of internal improvement, when I took my seat there as a member from Massachusetts, in 1823. But this is not all; we had a bill before us, and passed it in that house, entitled "An act to procure the necessary surveys, plans, and estimates upon the subject of roads and canals." *It authorized the president to cause surveys and estimates to be made of the routes of such roads and canals as he might deem of national importance in a commercial or military point of view, or for the transportation of the mail;* and appropriated thirty thousand dollars out of the treasury to defray the expense. This act, though preliminary in its nature, covered the whole ground. It took for granted the complete power of internal improvement, as far as any of its advocates had ever contended for it. Having passed the other house, the bill came up to the Senate, and was here considered and debated in April, 1824. The honorable member from South Carolina was a member of the Senate at that time. While the bill was under consideration here, a motion was made to add the following proviso : —

" *Provided,* That nothing herein contained shall be construed to affirm or *admit* a power in Congress, on their own authority, to make roads or canals within any of the states of the Union."

The yeas and nays were taken on this proviso, and the honorable member voted *in the negative.* The proviso failed.

A motion was then made to add this provision, viz. : —

" *Provided,* That the faith of the United States is hereby pledged, that no money shall ever be expended for roads or canals, except it shall be among the several states, and in the same proportion as direct taxes are laid and assessed by the provisions of the constitution."

The honorable member voted *against this proviso* also, and it failed.

The bill was then put on its passage, and the honorable member voted *for it,* and it passed, and became a law.

Now, it strikes me, sir, that there is no maintaining these votes but upon the power of internal improvement, in its broadest sense. In truth, these bills for surveys and estimates have always been considered as test questions. They show who is for and who against internal improvement. This law itself went the whole length, and assumed the full and complete power. The gentleman's votes sustained that power, in every form in which the various propositions to amend presented it. He went for the entire and unrestrained authority, without consulting the states, and without agreeing to any proportionate distribution. And now, suffer me to remind you, Mr. President, that it is this very same power, thus sanctioned, in every form, by the gentleman's own opinion, that is so plain and manifest a usurpation, that the state of South Carolina is supposed to be justified in refusing submission to any laws carrying the power into effect. Truly, sir, is not this a little too hard? May we not crave some mercy, under favor and protection of the gentleman's own authority? Admitting that a road or a canal must be written down flat usurpation as ever was committed, may we find no mitigation in our respect for his place, and his vote, as one that knows the law?

The tariff which South Carolina had an efficient hand in establishing in 1816, and this asserted power of internal improvement, — advanced by her in the same year, and, as we have now seen, approved and sanctioned by her representatives in 1824, — these two measures are the great grounds on which she is now thought to be justified in breaking up the Union, if she sees fit to break it up.

I may now safely say, I think, that we have had the authority of leading and distinguished gentlemen from South Carolina in support of the doctrine of internal improvement. I repeat, that, up to 1824, I, for one, followed South Carolina; but when that star in its ascension veered off in an unexpected direction, I relied on its light no longer. [Here the Vice President said, Does the Chair understand the gentleman from Massachusetts to say that the person now occupying the chair of the Senate has changed his opinions on the subject of internal improvements?] From nothing ever said to me, sir, have I had reason to know of any change in the opinions of the person filling the chair of the Senate. If such change has taken place, I regret it; I speak generally of the state of South Carolina. Individuals we know there are who hold opinions favorable to the power. An application for its exercise in behalf of a public work in South Carolina itself is now pending, I believe, in the other house, presented by members from that state.

I have thus, sir, perhaps not without some tediousness of detail, shown that, if I am in error on the subject of internal improvements, how and in what company I fell into that error. If I am wrong, it is apparent who misled me.

I go to other remarks of the honorable member — and I have to complain of an entire misapprehension of what I said on the subject of the national debt — though I can hardly perceive how any one could misunderstand me. What I said was, not that I wished to put off the payment of the debt, but, on the contrary, that I had always voted for every measure for its reduction, as uniformly as the gentleman himself. He seems to claim the exclusive merit of a disposition to reduce the public charge; I do not allow it to him. As a debt, I was, I am, for paying it; because it is a charge on our finances, and on the industry of the country. But I observed that I thought I perceived a morbid fervor on that subject; an excessive anxiety to pay off the debt; not so much because it is a debt simply, as because, while it lasts, it furnishes one objection to disunion. It is a tie of common interest while it lasts. I did not impute such motive to the honorable member himself; but that there is such a feeling in existence I have not a particle of doubt. The most I said was, that if one effect of the debt was to strengthen our Union, that effect itself was not regretted by me, however much others might regret it. The gentleman has not seen how to reply to this otherwise than by supposing me to have advanced the doctrine that a national debt is a national blessing. Others, I must hope, will find less difficulty in understanding me. I distinctly and pointedly cautioned the honorable member not to understand me as expressing an opinion favorable to the continuance of the debt. I repeated this caution, and repeated it more than once — but it was thrown away.

On yet another point I was still more unaccountably misunderstcod. The gentleman had harangued against "consolidation." I told him, in reply, that there was one kind of consolidation to which I was attached, and that was, the CONSOLIDATION OF OUR UNION; and that this was precisely that consolidation to which I feared others were not attached; that such consolidation was the very end of the constitution — the leading object, as they had informed us themselves, which its framers had kept in view. I turned to their communication, and read their very words, — "the consolidation of the Union," — and expressed my devotion to this sort of consolidation. I said in terms that I wished not, in the slightest degree, to augment the powers of this government; that my object was to preserve, not to enlarge; and that, by consolidating the Union, I understood no more than the strengthening of the Union and perpetuating it. Having been thus explicit; having thus read, from the printed book, the precise words which I adopted, as expressing my own sentiments, it passes comprehension, how any man could understand me as contending for an extension of the powers of the government, or for consolidation in that odious sense in which it means an accumulation, in the federal government, of the powers properly belonging to the states.

I repeat, sir, that, in adopting the sentiments of the framers of the constitution, I read their language audibly, and word for word; and I pointed out the distinction, just as fully as I have now done, between the consolidation of the Union and that other obnoxious consolidation which I disclaimed: and yet the honorable gentleman misunderstood me. The gentleman had said that he wished for no fixed revenue — not a shilling. If, by a word, he could convert the Capitol into gold, he would not do it. Why all this fear of revenue? Why, sir, because, as the gentleman told us, it tends to consolidation. Now, this can mean neither more nor less than that a common revenue is a common interest, and that all common interests tend to hold the union of the states together. I confess I like that tendency; if the gentleman dislikes it, he is right in deprecating a shilling's fixed revenue. So much, sir, for consolidation.

As well as I recollect the course of his remarks, the honorable gentleman next recurred to the subject of the tariff. He did not doubt the word must be of unpleasant sound to me, and proceeded, with an effort neither new nor attended with new success, to involve me and my votes in inconsistency and contradiction. I am happy the honorable gentleman has furnished me an opportunity of a timely remark or two on that subject. I was glad he approached it, for it is a question I enter upon without fear from any body. The strenuous toil of the gentleman has been to raise an inconsistency between my dissent to the tariff in 1824 and my vote in 1828. It is labor lost. He pays undeserved compliment to my speech in 1824; but this is to raise me high, that my fall, as he would have it, in 1828 may be the more signal. Sir, there was no fall at all. Between the ground I stood on in 1824 and that I took in 1828, there was not only no precipice, but no declivity. It was a change of position, to meet new circumstances, but on the same level. A plain tale explains the whole matter. In 1816, I had not acquiesced in the tariff, then supported by South Carolina. To some parts of it, especially, I felt and expressed great repugnance. I held the same opinions in 1821, at the meeting in Faneuil Hall, to which the gentleman has alluded. I said then, and say now, that, as an original question, the authority of Congress to exercise the revenue power, with direct reference to the protection of manufactures, is a questionable authority, far more questionable, in my judgment, than the power of internal improvements. I must confess, sir, that, in one respect, some impression has been made on my opinions lately. Mr. Madison's publication has put the power in a very strong light. He has placed it, I must acknowledge, upon grounds of construction and argument which seem impregnable. But, even if the power were doubtful, on the face of the constitution itself, it had been assumed and asserted in the first revenue law ever passed under that same constitution ; and, on this ground, as a matter settled by contemporaneous practice, I had refrained from expressing the opinion that the tariff laws transcended constitutional limits, as the gentleman supposes. What I did say at Faneuil Hall, as far as I now remember, was, that this was originally matter of doubtful construction. The gentleman himself, I suppose, thinks there is no doubt about it, and that the laws are plainly against the constitution. Mr. Madison's letters, already referred to, contain, in my judgment, by far the most able exposition extant of this part of the constitution. He has satisfied me, so far as the practice of the government had left it an open question.

With a great majority of the representatives of Massachusetts, I voted against the tariff of 1824. My reasons were then given, and I will not now repeat them. But notwithstanding our dissent, the great states of New York, Pennsylvania, Ohio, and Kentucky went for the bill, in almost unbroken column, and it passed. Congress and the president sanctioned it, and it became the law of the land. What, then, were we to do? Our only option was either to fall in with this settled course of public policy, and to accommodate ourselves to it as well as we could, or to embrace the South Carolina doctrine, and talk of nullifying the statute by state interference.

This last alternative did not suit our principles, and, of course, we adopted the former. In 1827, the subject came again before Congress, on a proposition favorable to wool and woollens. We looked upon the system of protection as being fixed and settled. The law of 1824 remained. It had gone into full operation, and in regard to some objects intended by it, perhaps most of them had produced all its expected effects. No man proposed to repeal it — no man attempted to renew the general contest on its principle. But, owing to subsequent and unforeseen occurrences, the benefit intended by it to wool and woollen fabrics had not been realized. Events, not known here when the law passed, had taken place, which defeated its object in that particular respect. A measure was accordingly brought forward to meet this precise deficiency, to remedy this particular defect. It was limited to wool and woollens. Was ever any thing more reasonable? If the policy of the tariff laws had become established in principle as the permanent policy of the government, should they not be revised and amended, and made equal, like other laws, as exigencies should arise, or justice require? Because we had doubted about adopting the system, were we to refuse to cure its manifest defects after it became adopted, and when no one attempted its repeal? And this, sir, is the inconsistency so much bruited. I had voted against the tariff of 1824 — but it passed ; and in 1827 and 1828, I voted to amend it in a point essential to the interest of my constituents. Where is the inconsistency? Could I do otherwise?

Sir, does political consistency consist in always giving negative votes? Does it require of a public man to refuse to concur in amending laws

because they passed against his consent? Having voted against the tariff
orginally, does consistency demand that I should do all in my power to
maintain an unequal tariff, burdensome to my own constituents, in many
respects, — favorable in none? To consistency of that sort I lay no
claim ; and there is another sort to which I lay as little — and that is, a
kind of consistency by which persons feel themselves as much bound to
oppose a proposition after it has become the law of the land as before.

The bill of 1827, limited, as I have said, to the single object in which
the tariff of 1824 had manifestly failed in its effect, passed the House of
Representatives, but was lost here. We had then the act of 1828. I
need not recur to the history of a measure so recent. Its enemies spiced
it with whatsoever they thought would render it distasteful; its friends
took it, drugged as it was. Vast amounts of property, many millions, had
been invested in manufactures, under the inducements of the act of 1824.
Events called loudly, as I thought, for further regulations to secure the
degree of protection intended by that act. I was disposed to vote for
such regulations, and desired nothing more ; but certainly was not to be
bantered out of my purpose by a threatened augmentation of duty on
molasses, put into the bill for the avowed purpose of making it obnoxious.
The vote may have been right or wrong, wise or unwise ; but it is little less
than absurd to allege against it an inconsistency with opposition to the
former law.

Sir, as to the general subject of the tariff, I have little now to say.
Another opportunity may be presented. I remarked, the other day, that
this policy did not begin with us in New England; and yet, sir, New
England is charged with vehemence as being favorable, or charged with
equal vehemence as being unfavorable, to the tariff policy, just as best
suits the time, place, and occasion for making some charge against her.
The credulity of the public has been put to its extreme capacity of false
impression relative to her conduct in this particular. Through all the
south, during the late contest, it was New England policy, and a New
England administration, that was afflicting the country with a tariff policy
beyond all endurance, while on the other side of the Alleghany, even
the act of 1828 itself — the very sublimated essence of oppression,
according to southern opinions — was pronounced to be one of those blessings for which the west was indebted to the "generous south."

With large investments in manufacturing establishments, and various
interests connected with and dependent on them, it is not to be expected
that New England, any more than other portions of the country, will now
consent to any measure destructive or highly dangerous. The duty of
the government, at the present moment, would seem to be to preserve,
not to destroy ; to maintain the position which it has assumed ; and for
one, I shall feel it an indispensable obligation to hold it steady, as far as
in my power, to that degree of protection which it has undertaken to
bestow. No more of the tariff.

Professing to be provoked by what he chose to consider a charge
made by me against South Carolina, the honorable member, Mr. President, has taken up a new crusade against New England. Leaving altogether the subject of the public lands, in which his success, perhaps, had
been neither distinguished nor satisfactory, and letting go, also, of the topic
of the tariff, he sallied forth in a general assault on the opinions, politics,
and parties of New England, as they have been exhibited in the last
thirty years, This is natural. The "narrow policy" of the public lands

had proved a legal settlement in South Carolina, and was not to be
removed. The "accursed policy" of the tariff, also, had established the
fact of its birth and parentage in the same state. No wonder, therefore,
the gentleman wished to carry the war, as he expressed it, into the
enemy's country. Prudently willing to quit these subjects, he was doubtless desirous of fastening others, which could not be transferred south of
Mason and Dixon's line. The politics of New England became his
theme ; and it was in this part of his speech, I think, that he menaced
me with such sore discomfiture.

Discomfiture ! why, sir, when he attacks any thing which I maintain,
and overthrows it ; when he turns the right or left of any position which
I take up ; when he drives me from any ground I choose to occupy, he
may then talk of discomfiture, but not till that distant day. What has he
done ? Has he maintained his own charges ? Has he proved what he
alleged ? Has he sustained himself in his attack on the government, and
on the history of the north, in the matter of the public lands ? Has he
disproved a fact, refuted a proposition, weakened an argument maintained
by me ? Has he come within beat of drum of any position of mine ?
O, no ; but he has "carried the war into the enemy's country" ! Carried
the war into the enemy's country ! Yes, sir, and what sort of a war has
he made of it ? Why, sir, he has stretched a dragnet over the whole
surface of perished pamphlets, indiscreet sermons, frothy paragraphs, and
fuming popular addresses ; over whatever the pulpit in its moments of
alarm, the press in its heats, and parties in their extravagance, have
severally thrown off, in times of general excitement and violence. He
has thus swept together a mass of such things, as, but that they are now
old, the public health would have required him rather to leave in their
state of dispersion.

For a good long hour or two, we had the unbroken pleasure of listening to the honorable member, while he recited, with his usual grace and
spirit, and with evident high gusto, speeches, pamphlets, addresses, and
all the *et ceteras* of the political press, such as warm heads produce in
warm times, and such as it would be "discomfiture" indeed for any one,
whose taste did not delight in that sort of reading, to be obliged to peruse.
This is his war. This is to carry the war into the enemy's country. It
is an invasion of this sort that he flatters himself with the expectation
of gaining laurels fit to adorn a senator's brow.

Mr. President, I shall not, it will, I trust, not be expected that I should,
either now or at any time, separate this farrago into parts, and answer
and examine its components. I shall hardly bestow upon it all a general
remark or two. In the run of forty years, sir, under this constitution,
we have experienced sundry successive violent party contests. Party
arose, indeed, with the constitution itself, and in some form or other has
attended through the greater part of its history.

Whether any other constitution than the old articles of confederation
was desirable was, itself, a question on which parties formed ; if a new
constitution was framed, what powers should be given to it was another
question ; and when it had been formed, what was, in fact, the just extent
of the powers actually conferred, was a third. Parties, as we know,
existed under the first administration, as distinctly marked as those which
manifested themselves at any subsequent period.

The contest immediately preceding the political change in 1801, and
that, again, which existed at the commencement of the late war, are other

instances of party excitement, of something more than usual strength and intensity. In all these conflicts there was, no doubt, much of violence on both and all sides. It would be impossible, if one had a fancy for such employment, to adjust the relative *quantum* of violence between these two contending parties. There was enough in each, as must always be expected in popular governments. With a great deal of proper and decorous discussion there was mingled a great deal, also, of declamation, virulence, crimination, and abuse.

In regard to any party, probably, at one of the leading epochs in the history of parties, enough may be found to make out another equally inflamed exhibition as that with which the honorable member has edified us. For myself, sir, I shall not rake among the rubbish of by-gone times to see what I can find, or whether I cannot find something by which I can fix a blot on the escutcheon of any state, any party, or any part of the country. General Washington's administration was steadily and zealously maintained, as we all know, by New England. It was violently opposed elsewhere. We know in what quarter he had the most earnest, constant, and persevering support, in all his great and leading measures. We know where his private and personal character were held in the highest degree of attachment and veneration; and we know, too, where his measures were opposed, his services slighted, and his character vilified.

We know, or we might know, if we turn to the journals, who expressed respect, gratitude, and regret, when he retired from the chief magistracy; and who refused to express either respect, gratitude, or regret. I shall not open those journals. Publications more abusive or scurrilous never saw the light than were sent forth against Washington, and all his leading measures, from presses south of New England; but I shall not look them up. I employ no scavengers — no one is in attendance on me, tendering such means of retaliation; and if there were, with an ass's load of them, with a bulk as huge as that which the gentleman himself has produced, I would not touch one of them. I see enough of the violence of our own times to be no way anxious to rescue from forgetfulness the extravagances of times past. Besides, what is all this to the present purpose? It has nothing to do with the public lands, in regard to which the attack was begun; and it has nothing to do with those sentiments and opinions, which I have thought tend to disunion, and all of which the honorable member seems to have adopted himself, and undertaken to defend. New England has, at times, — so argues the gentleman, — held opinions as dangerous as those which he now holds. Be it so. But why, therefore, does he abuse New England? If he finds himself countenanced by acts of hers, how is it that, while he relies on these acts, he covers, or seeks to cover, their authors with reproach?

But, sir, if, in the course of forty years, there have been undue effervescences of party in New England, has the same thing happened nowhere else? Party animosity and party outrage, not in New England, but elsewhere, denounced President Washington, not only as a federalist, but as a tory, a British agent, a man who, in his high office, sanctioned corruption. But does the honorable member suppose that, if I had a tender here, who should put such an effusion of wickedness and folly in my hand, that I would stand up and read it against the south? Parties ran into great heats, again, in 1799 and 1800. What was said, sir, or rather what was not said, in those years, against John Adams, one of the

5

signers of the Declaration of Independence, and its admitted ablest defender on the floor of Congress? If the gentleman wants to increase his stores of party abuse and frothy violence, if he has a determined proclivity to such pursuits, there are treasures of that sort south of the Potomac, much to his taste, yet untouched. I shall not touch them.

The parties which divided the country, at the commencement of the late war, were violent. But, then, there was violence on both sides, and violence in every state. Minorities and majorities were equally violent. There was no more violence against the war in New England than in other states; nor any more appearance of violence, except that, owing to a dense population, greater facility for assembling, and more presses, there may have been more, in quantity, spoken and printed there than in some other places. In the article of sermons, too, New England is somewhat more abundant than South Carolina; and for that reason, the chance of finding here and there an exceptionable one may be greater. I hope, too, there are more good ones. Opposition may have been more formidable in New England, as it embraced a larger portion of the whole population; but it was no more unrestrained in its principle, or violent in manner. The minorities dealt quite as harshly with their own state governments as the majorities dealt with the administration here. There were presses on both sides, popular meetings on both sides, ay, and pulpits on both sides, also. The gentleman's purveyors have only catered for him among the productions of one side. I certainly shall not supply the deficiency by furnishing samples of the other. I leave to him, and to them, the whole concern.

It is enough for me to say, that if, in any part of this, their grateful occupation — if in all their researches — they find any thing in the history of Massachusetts, or New England, or in the proceedings of any legislative or other public body, disloyal to the Union, speaking slightly of its value, proposing to break it up, or recommending non-intercourse with neighboring states, on account of difference of political opinion, then, sir, I give them all up to the honorable gentleman's unrestrained rebuke; expecting, however, that he will extend his buffetings, in like manner, to all similar proceedings, wherever else found.

The gentleman, sir, has spoken at large of former parties, now no longer in being, by their received appellations, and has undertaken to instruct us, not only in the knowledge of their principles, but of their respective pedigrees also. He has ascended to their origin, and run out their genealogies. With most exemplary modesty, he speaks of the party to which he professes to have belonged himself, as the true, pure, the only honest, patriotic party, derived by regular descent, from father to son, from the time of the virtuous Romans! Spreading before us the family tree of political parties, he takes especial care to show himself snugly perched on a popular bough! He is wakeful to the expediency of adopting such rules of descent, for political parties, as shall bring him in, in exclusion of others, as an heir to the inheritance of all public virtue, and all true political principles. His doxy is always orthodoxy. Heterodoxy is confined to his opponents. He spoke, sir, of the federalists, and I thought I saw some eyes begin to open and stare a little, when he ventured on that ground. I expected he would draw his sketches rather lightly, when he looked on the circle round him, and especially if he should cast his thoughts to the high places out of the Senate. Nevertheless, he went back to Rome, *ad annum urbe condita,* and found the fathers of the federalist in the primeval aristocrats of that renowned empire! He traced the flow of federal blood down through successive ages and centuries, till he got into the veins of the American tories, (of whom, by the way, there were twenty in the Carolinas for one in Massachusetts.) From the tories, he followed it to the federalists; and as the federal party was broken up, and there was no possibility of transmitting it farther on this side of the Atlantic, he seems to have discovered that it has gone off, collaterally, though against all the canons of descent, into the ultras of France, and finally became extinguished, like exploded gas, among the adherents of Don Miguel.

This, sir, is an abstract of the gentleman's history of federalism. I am not about to controvert it. It is not, at present, worth the pains of refutation, because, sir, if at this day one feels the sin of federalism lying heavily on his conscience, he can easily obtain remission. He may even have an indulgence, if he is desirous of repeating the transgression. It is an affair of no difficulty to get into this same right line of patriotic descent. A man, nowadays, is at liberty to choose his political parentage. He may elect his own father. Federalist or not, he may, if he choose, claim to belong to the favored stock, and his claim will be allowed. He may carry back his pretensions just as far as the honorable gentleman himself; nay, he may make himself out the honorable gentleman's cousin, and prove satisfactorily that he is descended from the same political great-grandfather. All this is allowable. We all know a process, sir, by which the whole Essex Junto could, in one hour, be all washed white from their ancient federalism, and come out, every one of them, an original democrat, dyed in the wool! Some of them have actually undergone the operation, and they say it is quite easy. The only inconvenience it occasions, as they tell us, is a slight tendency of the blood to the face, a soft suffusion, which, however, is very transient, since nothing is said calculated to deepen the red on the cheek, but a prudent silence observed in regard to all the past. Indeed, sir, some smiles of approbation have been bestowed, and some crums of comfort have fallen, not a thousand miles from the door of the Hartford Convention itself. And if the author of the ordinance of 1787 possessed the other requisite qualifications, there is no knowing, notwithstanding his federalism, to what heights of favor he might not yet attain.

Mr. President, in carrying his warfare, such as it was, into New England, the honorable gentleman all along professes to be acting on the defensive. He desires to consider me as having assailed South Carolina, and insists that he comes forth only as her champion, and in her defence. Sir, I do not admit that I made any attack whatever on South Carolina. Nothing like it. The honorable member, in his first speech, expressed opinions, in regard to revenue, and some other topics, which I heard both with pain and surprise. I told the gentleman that I was aware that such sentiments were entertained OUT of the government, but had not expected to find them advanced in it; that I knew there were persons in the south who speak of our Union with indifference, or doubt, taking pains to magnify its evils, and to say nothing of its benefits; that the honorable member himself, I was sure, could never be one of these; and I regretted the expression of such opinions as he had avowed, because I thought their obvious tendency was to encourage feelings of disrespect to the Union, and to weaken its connection. This, sir, is the sum and substance of all I said on the subject And this constitutes the attack which called on the chivalry of the gentleman, in his opinion, to harry us with such a forage among the party pamphlets and party proceedings of Massachusetts. If he means that I spoke with dissatisfaction or disrespect of the ebullitions of individuals in South Carolina, it is true. But, if he means that I had assailed the character of the state, her honor, or patriotism, that I had reflected on her history or her conduct, he had not the slightest ground for any such assumption. I did not even refer, I think, in my observations, to any collection of individuals. I said nothing of the recent conventions. I spoke in the most guarded and careful manner, and only expressed my regret for the publication of opinions which I presumed the honorable member disapproved as much as myself. In this, it seems, I was mistaken.

I do not remember that the gentleman has disclaimed any sentiment, or any opinion, of a supposed anti-Union tendency, which on all or any of the recent occasions has been expressed. The whole drift of his speech has been rather to prove, that, in divers times and manners, sentiments equally liable to objection have been promulgated in New England. And one would suppose that his object, in this reference to Massachusetts, was to find a precedent to justify proceedings in the south, were it not for the reproach and contumely with which he labors, all along, to load his precedents.

By way of defending South Carolina from what he chooses to think an attack on her, he first quotes the example of Massachusetts, and then denounces that example, in good set terms. This twofold purpose, not very consistent with itself, one would think, was exhibited more than once in the course of his speech. He referred, for instance, to the Hartford Convention. Did he do this for authority, or for a topic of reproach? Apparently for both; for he told us that he should find no fault with the mere fact of holding such a convention, and considering and discussing such questions as he supposes were then and there discussed; but what rendered it obnoxious was the time it was holden, and the circumstances of the country then existing. We were in a war, he said, and the country needed all our aid; the hand of government required to be strengthened, not weakened; and patriotism should have postponed such proceedings to another day. The thing itself, then, is a precedent; the time and manner of it, only, subject of censure.

Now, sir, I go much farther, on this point, than the honorable member. Supposing, as the gentleman seems to, that the Hartford Convention assembled for any such purpose as breaking up the Union, because they thought unconstitutional laws had been passed, or to concert on that subject, or to calculate the value of the Union; supposing this to be their purpose, or any part of it, then I say the meeting itself was disloyal, and obnoxious to censure, whether held in time of peace, or time of war, or under whatever circumstances. The material matter is the object. Is dissolution the object? If it be, external circumstances may make it a more or less aggravated case, but cannot affect the principle. I do not hold, therefore, that the Hartford Convention was pardonable, even to the extent of the gentleman's admission, if its objects were really such as have been imputed to it. Sir, there never was a time, under any degree of excitement, in which the Hartford Convention, or any other convention, could maintain itself one moment in New England, if assembled for any such purpose as the gentleman says would have been an allowable purpose. To hold conventions to decide questions of constitutional law! —

to try the binding validity of statutes, by votes in a convention! Sir, the Hartford Convention, I presume, would not desire that the honorable gentleman should be their defender or advocate, if he puts their case upon such untenable and extravagant grounds.

Then, sir, the gentleman has no fault to find with these recently-promulgated South Carolina opinions. And, certainly, he need have none ; for his own sentiments, as now advanced, and advanced on reflection, as far as I have been able to comprehend them, go the full length of all these opinions. I propose, sir, to say something on these, and to consider how far they are just and constitutional. Before doing that, however, let me observe, that the eulogium pronounced on the character of the state of South Carolina, by the honorable gentleman, for her revolutionary and other merits, meets my hearty concurrence. I shall not acknowledge that the honorable member goes before me in regard for whatever of distinguished talent or distinguished character South Carolina has produced. I claim part of the honor, I partake in the pride, of her great names. I claim them for countrymen, one and all. The Laurenses, the Rutledges, the Pinckneys, the Sumpters, the Marions — Americans all — whose fame is no more to be hemmed in by state lines than their talents and patriotism were capable of being circumscribed within the same narrow limits. In their day and generation, they served and honored the country, and the whole country ; and their renown is of the treasures of the whole country. Him whose honored name the gentleman himself bears — does he suppose me less capable of gratitude for his patriotism, or sympathy for his sufferings, than if his eyes had first opened upon the light in Massachusetts instead of South Carolina? Sir, does he suppose it is in his power to exhibit a Carolina name so bright as to produce envy in my bosom? No, sir, increased gratification and delight, rather.

Sir, I thank God that if I am gifted with little of the spirit which is said to be able to raise mortals to the skies, I have yet none, as I trust, of that other spirit, which would drag angels down. When I shall be found, sir, in my place here in the Senate, or elsewhere, to sneer at public merit, because it happened to spring up beyond the little limits of my own state, or neighborhood ; when I refuse, for any such cause, or for any cause, the homage due to American talent, to elevated patriotism, to sincere devotion to liberty and the country ; or if I see an uncommon endowment of Heaven, if I see extraordinary capacity and virtue in any son of the south, and if, moved by local prejudice, or gangrened by state jealousy, I get up here to abate the tithe of a hair from his just character and just fame, — may my tongue cleave to the roof of my mouth! Sir, let me recur to pleasing recollections ; let me indulge in refreshing remembrance of the past ; let me remind you that in early times no states cherished greater harmony, both of principle and feeling, than Massachusetts and South Carolina. Would to God that harmony might again return. Shoulder to shoulder they went through the revolution ; hand in hand they stood round the administration of Washington, and felt his own great arm lean on them for support. Unkind feeling, if it exist, alienation, and distrust are the growth, unnatural to such soils, of false principles since sown. They are weeds, the seeds of which that same great arm never scattered.

Mr. President, I shall enter on no encomium upon Massachusetts — she needs none. There she is — behold her, and judge for yourselves. There is her history — the world knows it by heart. The past, at least, is secure. There is Boston, and Concord, and Lexington, and Bunker Hill; and there they will remain forever. The bones of her sons, fallen in the great struggle for independence, now lie mingled with the soil of every state from New England to Georgia; and there they will lie forever. And, sir, where American liberty raised its first voice, and where its youth was nurtured and sustained, there it still lives, in the strength of its manhood, and full of its original spirit. If discord and disunion shall wound it; if party strife and blind ambition shall hawk at and tear it; if folly and madness, if uneasiness under salutary and necessary restraint, shall succeed to separate it from that Union by which alone its existence is made sure, — it will stand, in the end, by the side of that cradle in which its infancy was rocked; it will stretch forth its arm, with whatever vigor it may still retain, over the friends who gather round it; and it will fall at last, if fall it must, amidst the proudest monuments of its own glory, and on the very spot of its origin.

There yet remains to be performed, Mr. President, by far the most grave and important duty which I feel to be devolved on me by this occasion. It is to state, and to defend, what I conceive to be the true principles of the constitution under which we are here assembled. I might well have desired that so weighty a task should have fallen into other and abler hands. I could have wished that it should have been executed by those whose character and experience give weight and influence to their opinions, such as cannot possibly belong to mine. But, sir, I have met the occasion, not sought it; and I shall proceed to state my own sentiments, without challenging for them any particular regard, with studied plainness and as much precision as possible.

I understand the honorable gentleman from South Carolina to maintain that it is a right of the state legislatures to interfere, whenever, in their judgment, this government transcends its constitutional limits, and to arrest the operation of its laws.

I understand him to maintain this right as a right existing *under* the constitution, not as a right to overthrow it, on the ground of extreme necessity, such as would justify violent revolution.

I understand him to maintain an authority, on the part of the states, thus to interfere, for the purpose of correcting the exercise of power by the general government, of checking it, and of compelling it to conform to their opinion of the extent of its power.

I understand him to maintain that the ultimate power of judging of the constitutional extent of its own authority is not lodged exclusively in the general government or any branch of it; but that, on the contrary, the states may lawfully decide for themselves, and each state for itself, whether, in a given case, the act of the general government transcends its power.

I understand him to insist that, if the exigency of the case, in the opinion of any state government, require it, such state government may, by its own sovereign authority, annul an act of the general government which it deems plainly and palpably unconstitutional.

This is the sum of what I understand from him to be the South Carolina doctrine. I propose to consider it, and to compare it with the constitution. Allow me to say, as a preliminary remark, that I call this the South Carolina doctrine, only because the gentleman himself has so denominated it. I do not feel at liberty to say that South Carolina, as a state, has ever advanced these sentiments. I hope she has not, and never may. That a great majority of her people are opposed to the tariff laws is doubtless true. That a majority, somewhat less than that just mentioned, conscientiously believe these laws unconstitutional, may probably also be true. But that any majority holds to the right of direct state interference, at state discretion, the right of nullifying acts of Congress by acts of state legislation, is more than I know, and what I shall be slow to believe.

That there are individuals, besides the honorable gentleman, who do maintain these opinions, is quite certain. I recollect the recent expression of a sentiment which circumstances attending its utterance and publication justify us in supposing was not unpremeditated — " The sovereignty of the state : never to be controlled, construed, or decided on, but by her own feelings of honorable justice."

[Mr. HAYNE here rose, and said, that, for the purpose of being clearly understood, he would state that his proposition was in the words of the Virginia resolution, as follows : —

" That this Assembly doth explicitly and peremptorily declare, that it views the powers of the federal government, as resulting from the compact, to which the states are parties, as limited by the plain sense and intention of the instrument constituting that compact, as no further valid than they are authorized by the grants enumerated in that compact ; and that, in case of a deliberate, palpable, and dangerous exercise of other powers not granted by the said compact, the states who are parties thereto have the right, and are in duty bound, to interpose for arresting the progress of the evil, and for maintaining, within their respective limits, the authorities, rights, and liberties pertaining to them."]

Mr. WEBSTER resumed : —

I am quite aware, Mr. President, of the existence of the resolution which the gentleman read, and has now repeated, and that he relies on it as his authority. I know the source, too, from which it is understood to have proceeded. I need not say, that I have much respect for the constitutional opinions of Mr. Madison : they would weigh greatly with me, always. But, before the authority of his opinion be vouched for the gentleman's proposition, it will be proper to consider what is the fair interpretation of that resolution, to which Mr. Madison is understood to have given his sanction. As the gentleman construes it, it is an authority for him. Possibly he may not have adopted the right construction. That resolution declares, *that in the case of the dangerous exercise of powers not granted by the general government, the states may interpose to arrest the progress of the evil.* But how interpose ? and what does this declaration purport ? Does it mean no more than that there may be extreme cases in which the people, in any mode of assembling, may resist usurpation, and relieve themselves from a tyrannical government? No one will deny this. Such resistance is not only acknowledged to be just in America, but in England also. Blackstone admits as much, in the theory and practice, too, of the English constitution. We, sir, who oppose he Carolina doctrine, do not deny that the people may, if they choose, throw off any government, when it becomes oppressive and intolerable, and erect a better in its stead. We all know that civil institutions are established for the public benefit, and that, when they cease to answer the ends of their existence, they may be changed.

But I do not understand the doctrine now contended for to be that which, for the sake of distinctness, we may call the right of revolution.

I understand the gentleman to maintain, that without revolution, **without**
civil commotion, without rebellion, a remedy for supposed abuse and
transgression of the powers of the general government lies in a direct
appeal to the interference of the state governments. [Mr. HAYNE here
rose : He did not contend, he said, for the mere right of revolution, but
for the right of constitutional resistance. What he maintained was, that,
in case of a plain, palpable violation of the constitution by the general
government, a state may interpose ; and that this interposition is constitutional.] Mr. WEBSTER resumed : —

So, sir, I understood the gentleman, and am happy to find that I did
not misunderstand him. What he contends for is, that it is constitutional
to interrupt the administration of the constitution itself, in the hands of
those who are chosen and sworn to administer it, by the direct interference, in form of law, of the states, in virtue of their sovereign capacity.
The inherent right in the people to reform their government I do not
deny ; and they have another right, and that is, to resist unconstitutional
laws, without overturning the government. It is no doctrine of mine, that
unconstitutional laws bind the people. The great question is, *Whose prerogative is it to decide on the constitutionality or unconstitutionality of the
laws ?* On that the main debate hinges. The proposition that, in case of
a supposed violation of the constitution by Congress, the states have a
constitutional right to interfere, and annul the law of Congress, is the
proposition of the gentleman ; I do not admit it. If the gentleman had
intended no more than to assert the right of revolution for justifiable cause,
he would have said only what all agree to. But I cannot conceive that
there can be a middle course between submission to the laws, when regu-
larly pronounced constitutional, on the one hand, and open resistance,
which is revolution or rebellion, on the other. I say the right of a state
to annul a law of Congress cannot be maintained but on the ground of
the unalienable right of man to resist oppression ; that is to say, upon the
ground of revolution. I admit that there is an ultimate violent remedy,
above the constitution, and in defiance of the constitution, which may be
resorted to, when a revolution is to be justified. But I do not admit that,
under the constitution, and in conformity with it, there is any mode in
which a state government, as a member of the Union, can interfere and
stop the progress of the general government, by force of her own laws,
under any circumstances whatever.

This leads us to inquire into the origin of this government, and the
source of its power. Whose agent is it ? Is it the creature of the state
legislatures, or the creature of the people ? If the government of the
United States be the agent of the state governments, then they may
control it, provided they can agree in the manner of controlling it ; if it is
the agent of the people, then the people alone can control it, restrain it,
modify or reform it. It is observable enough, that the doctrine for which
the honorable gentleman contends leads him to the necessity of maintaining, not only that this general government is the creature of the
states, but that it is the creature of each of the states severally ; so that
each may assert the power, for itself, of determining whether it acts
within the limits of its authority. It is the servant of four and twenty
masters, of different wills and different purposes ; and yet bound to obey
all. This absurdity (for it seems no less) arises from a misconception
as to the origin of this government, and its true character. It is, sir, the
people's constitution, the people's government ; made for the people ;

made by the people; and answerable to the people. The people of the United States have declared that this constitution shall be the supreme law. We must either admit the proposition, or dispute their authority. The states are unquestionably sovereign, so far as their sovereignty is not affected by this supreme law. The state legislatures, as political bodies, however sovereign, are yet not sovereign over the people. So far as the people have given power to the general government, so far the grant is unquestionably good, and the government holds of the people, and not of the state governments. We are all agents of the same supreme power, the people. The general government and the state governments derive their authority from the same source. Neither can, in relation to the other, be called primary; though one is definite and restricted, and the other general and residuary.

The national government possesses those powers which it can be shown the people have conferred on it, and no more. All the rest belongs to the state governments, or to the people themselves. So far as the people have restrained state sovereignty by the expression of their will, in the constitution of the United States, so far, it must be admitted, state sovereignty is effectually controlled. I do not contend that it is, or ought to be, controlled further. The sentiment to which I have referred propounds that state sovereignty is only to be controlled by its own "feeling of justice;" that is to say, it is not to be controlled at all; for one who is to follow his feelings, is under no legal control. Now, however men may think this ought to be, the fact is, that the people of the United States have chosen to impose control on state sovereignties. The constitution has ordered the matter differently from what this opinion announces. To make war, for instance, is an exercise of sovereignty; but the constitution declares that no state shall make war. To coin money is another exercise of sovereign power; but no state is at liberty to coin money. Again: the constitution says, that no sovereign state shall be so sovereign as to make a treaty. These prohibitions, it must be confessed, are a control on the state sovereignty of South Carolina, as well as of the other states, which does not arise "from her own feelings of honorable justice." Such an opinion, therefore, is in defiance of the plainest provisions of the constitution.

There are other proceedings of public bodies which have already been alluded to, and to which I refer again for the purpose of ascertaining more fully what is the length and breadth of that doctrine, denominated the Carolina doctrine, which the honorable member has now stood up on this floor to maintain.

In one of them I find it resolved that "the tariff of 1828, and every other tariff designed to promote one branch of industry at the expense of others, is contrary to the meaning and intention of the federal compact; and as such, a dangerous, palpable, and deliberate usurpation of power, by a determined majority, wielding the general government beyond the limits of its delegated powers, as calls upon the states which compose the suffering minority, in their sovereign capacity, to exercise the powers which, as sovereigns, necessarily devolve upon them, when their compact is violated."

Observe, sir, that this resolution holds the tariff of 1828, and every other tariff, designed to promote one branch of industry at the expense of another, to be such a dangerous, palpable, and deliberate usurpation of power, as calls upon the states, in their sovereign capacity, to interfere by their own power. This denunciation, Mr. President, you will please to observe, includes our old tariff of 1816, as well as all others ; because that was established to promote the interest of the manufactures of cotton, to the manifest and admitted injury of the Calcutta cotton trade. Observe, again, that all the qualifications are here rehearsed, and charged upon the tariff, which are necessary to bring the case within the gentleman's proposition. The tariff is a usurpation ; it is a dangerous usurpation ; it is a palpable usurpation ; it is a deliberate usurpation. It is such a usurpation as calls upon the states to exercise their right of interference. Here is a case, then, within the gentleman's principles, and all his qualifications of his principles. It is a case for action. The constitution is plainly, dangerously, palpably, and deliberately violated ; and the states must interpose their own authority to arrest the law. Let us suppose the state of South Carolina to express this same opinion, by the voice of her legislature. That would be very imposing ; but what then ? Is the voice of one state conclusive ? It so happens that, at the very moment when South Carolina resolves that the tariff laws are unconstitutional, Pennsylvania and Kentucky resolve exactly the reverse. *They* hold those laws to be both highly proper and strictly constitutional. And now, sir, how does the honorable member propose to deal with this case ? How does he get out of this difficulty, upon any principle of his ? His construction gets us into it ; how does he propose to get us out ?

In Carolina, the tariff is a palpable, deliberate usurpation ; Carolina, therefore, may *nullify* it, and refuse to pay the duties. In Pennsylvania, it is both clearly constitutional and highly expedient ; and there the duties are to be paid. And yet we live under a government of uniform laws, and under a constitution, too, which contains an express provision, as it happens, that all duties shall be equal in all the states ! Does not this approach absurdity ?

If there be no power to settle such questions, independent of either of the states, is not the whole Union a rope of sand ? Are we not thrown back again precisely upon the old confederation ?

It is too plain to be argued. Four and twenty interpreters of constitutional law, each with a power to decide for itself, and none with authority to bind any body else, and this constitutional law the only bond of their union ! What is such a state of things but a mere connection during pleasure, or, to use the phraseology of the times, *during feeling?* And that feeling, too, not the feeling of the people who established the constitution, but the feeling of the state governments.

In another of the South Carolina addresses, having premised that the crisis requires " all the concentrated energy of passion," an attitude of open resistance to the laws of the Union is advised. Open resistance to the laws, then, is the constitutional remedy, the conservative power of the state, which the South Carolina doctrines teach for the redress of political evils, real or imaginary. And its authors further say that, appealing with confidence to the constitution itself to justify their opinions, they cannot consent to try their accuracy by the courts of justice. In one sense, indeed, sir, this is assuming an attitude of open resistance in favor of liberty. But what sort of liberty ? The liberty of establishing their own opinions, in defiance of the opinions of all others ; the liberty of judging and of deciding exclusively themselves, in a matter in which others have as much right to judge and decide as they ; the liberty of placing their opinions above the judgment of all others, above the laws, and above the constitution. This is their liberty, and this is the fair result of the proposition contended for by the honorable gentleman. Or it may be more properly said, it is identical with it, rather than a result from it. In the same publication we find the following : " Previously to our revolution, when the arm of oppression was stretched over New England, where did our northern brethren meet with a braver sympathy than that which sprung from the bosom of Carolinians ? *We had no extortion, no oppression, no collision with the king's ministers, no navigation interests springing up, in envious rivalry of England.*"

This seems extraordinary language. South Carolina no collision with the king's ministers in 1775 ! no extortion ! no oppression ! But, sir, it is also most significant language. Does any man doubt the purpose for which it was penned ? Can any one fail to see that it was designed to raise in the reader's mind the question, whether, *at this time,* — that is to say, in 1828, — South Carolina has any collision with the king's ministers, any oppression, or extortion, to fear from England ? whether, in short, England is not as naturally the friend of South Carolina as New England, with her navigation interests springing up in envious rivalry of England?

Is it not strange, sir, that an intelligent man in South Carolina, in 1828, should thus labor to prove, that, in 1775, there was no hostility, no cause of war, between South Carolina and England ? that she had no occasion, in reference to her own interest, or from a regard to her own welfare, to take up arms in the revolutionary contest ? Can any one account for the expression of such strange sentiments, and their circulation through the state, otherwise than by supposing the object to be, what I have already intimated, to raise the question, if they had no " *collision* " (mark the expression) with the ministers of King George the Third, in 1775, what *collision* have they, in 1828, with the ministers of King George the Fourth ? What is there now, in the existing state of things, to separate Carolina from *Old,* more, or rather less, than from *New* England?

Resolutions, sir, have been recently passed by the legislature of South Carolina. I need not refer to them ; they go no further than the honorable gentleman himself has gone — and I hope not so far. I content myself, therefore, with debating the matter with him.

And now, sir, what I have first to say on this subject is, that at no time, and under no circumstances, has New England, or any state in New England, or any respectable body of persons in New England, or any public man of standing in New England, put forth such a doctrine as this Carolina doctrine.

The gentleman has found no case — he can find none — to support his own opinions by New England authority. New England has studied the constitution in other schools, and under other teachers. She looks upon it with other regards, and deems more highly and reverently, both of its just authority and its utility and excellence. The history of her legislative proceedings may be traced — the ephemeral effusions of temporary bodies, called together by the excitement of the occasion, may be hunted up — they have been hunted up. The opinions and votes of her public men, in and out of Congress, may be explored — it will all be in vain. The Carolina doctrine can derive from her neither countenance nor support. She rejects it now ; she always did reject it ; and till she loses her senses, she always will reject it. The honorable member has referred to expressions on the subject of the embargo law, made in this place by an honorable and venerable gentleman (Mr. HILLHOUSE) now favoring us with his presence. He quotes that distinguished senator as saying, that in his judgment the embargo law was unconstitutional, and that, therefore, in his opinion, the people were not bound to obey it.

That, sir, is perfectly constitutional language. An unconstitutional law is not binding ; *but then it does not rest with a resolution or a law of a state legislature to decide whether an act of Congress be or be not constitutional.* An unconstitutional act of Congress would not bind the people of this District, although they have no legislature to interfere in their behalf; and, on the other hand, a constitutional law of Congress does bind the citizens of every state, although all their legislatures should undertake to annul it, by act or resolution. The venerable Connecticut senator is a constitutional lawyer, of sound principles and enlarged knowledge ; a statesman practised and experienced, bred in the company of Washington, and holding just views upon the nature of our governments. He believed the embargo unconstitutional, and so did others ; but what then ? Who did he suppose was to decide that question ? The state legislatures ? Certainly not. No such sentiment ever escaped his lips. Let us follow up, sir, this New England opposition to the embargo laws ; let us trace it, till we discern the principle which controlled and governed New England throughout the whole course of that opposition. We shall then see what similarity there is between the New England school of constitutional opinions and this modern Carolina school. The gentleman, I think, read a petition from some single individual, addressed to the legislature of Massachusetts, asserting the Carolina doctrine — that is, the right of state interference to arrest the laws of the Union. The fate of that petition shows the sentiment of the legislature. It met no favor. The opinions of Massachusetts were otherwise. They had been expressed in 1798, in answer to the resolutions of Virginia, and she did not depart from them, nor bend them to the times. Misgoverned, wronged, oppressed, as she felt herself to be, she still held fast her integrity to the Union. The gentleman may find in her proceedings much evidence of dissatisfaction with the measures of government, and great and deep dislike to the embargo ; all this makes the case so much the stronger for her ; for, notwithstanding all this dissatisfaction and dislike, she claimed no right still to sever asunder the bonds of the Union. There was heat and there was anger in her political feeling. Be it so. Her heat or her anger did not, nevertheless, betray her into infidelity to the government. The gentleman labors to prove that she disliked the embargo as much as South Carolina dislikes the tariff, and expressed her dislike as strongly. Be it so ; *but did she propose the Carolina remedy ? Did she threaten to interfere, by state authority, to annul the laws of the Union ?* That is the question for the gentleman's consideration.

No doubt, sir, a great majority of the people of New England conscientiously believed the embargo law of 1807 unconstitutional — as conscientiously, certainly, as the people of South Carolina hold that opinion of the tariff. They reasoned thus : Congress has power to regulate commerce ; but here is a law, they said, stopping all commerce, and stopping it indefinitely. The law is perpetual; that is, it is not limited in point of time, and must of course continue till it shall be repealed by some other law. It is as perpetual, therefore, as the law against treason or murder. Now, is this regulating commerce, or destroying it ? Is it guiding, controlling, giving the rule to commerce, as a subsisting thing, or is it putting an end to it altogether ? Nothing is more certain than that a majority in

New England deemed this law a violation of the constitution. The very case required by the gentleman to justify state interference had then arisen. Massachusetts believed this law to be " *a deliberate, palpable, and dangerous exercise of a power not granted by the constitution.*" Deliberate it was, for it was long continued; palpable she thought it, as no words in the constitution gave the power, and only a construction, in her opinion most violent, raised it; dangerous it was, since it threatened utter ruin to her most important interests. Here, then, was a Carolina case. How did Massachusetts deal with it? It was, as she thought, a plain, manifest, palpable violation of the constitution; and it brought ruin to her doors. Thousands of families, and hundreds of thousands of individuals, were beggared by it. While she saw and felt all this, she saw and felt, also, that as a measure of national policy, it was perfectly futile; that the country was no way benefited by that which caused so much individual distress; that it was efficient only for the production of evil, and all that evil inflicted on ourselves. In such a case, under such circumstances, how did Massachusetts demean herself? Sir, she remonstrated, she memorialized, she addressed herself to the general government, not exactly " with the concentrated energy of passion," but with her strong sense, and the energy of sober conviction. But she did not interpose the arm of her power to arrest the law, and break the embargo. Far from it. Her principles bound her to two things; and she followed her principles, lead where they might. First, to submit to every constitutional law of Congress; and secondly, if the constitutional validity of the law be doubted, to refer that question to the decision of the proper tribunals. The first principle is vain and ineffectual without the second. A majority of us in New England believed the embargo law unconstitutional; but the great question was, and always will be, in such cases, Who is to decide this? Who is to judge between the people and the government? And, sir, it is quite plain, that the constitution of the United States confers on the government itself, to be exercised by its appropriate department, this power of deciding, ultimately and conclusively, upon the just extent of its own authority. If this had not been done, we should not have advanced a single step beyond the old confederation.

Being fully of opinion that the embargo law was unconstitutional, the people of New England were yet equally clear in the opinion — it was a matter they did not doubt upon — that the question, after all, must be decided by the judicial tribunals of the United States. Before those tribunals, therefore, they brought the question. Under the provisions of the law, they had given bonds, to millions in amount, and which were alleged to be forfeited. They suffered the bonds to be sued, and thus raised the question. In the old-fashioned way of settling disputes, they went to law The case came to hearing and solemn argument; and he who espoused their cause and stood up for them against the validity of the act, was none other than that great man, of whom the gentleman has made honorable mention, SAMUEL DEXTER. He was then, sir, in the fulness of his knowledge and the maturity of his strength. He had retired from long and distinguished public service here, to the renewed pursuit of professional duties; carrying with him all that enlargement and expansion, all the new strength and force, which an acquaintance with the more general subjects discussed in the national councils is capable of adding to professional attainment, in a mind of true greatness and comprehension.

He was a lawyer, and he was also a statesman. He had studied the con
stitution, when he filled public station, that he might defend it ; he had
examined its principles, that he might maintain them. More than all
men, or at least as much as any man, he was attached to the general
government, and to the union of the states. His feelings and opinions
all ran in that direction. A question of constitutional law, too, was, of
all subjects, that one which was best suited to his talents and learning.
Aloof from technicality, and unfettered by artificial rule, such a question
gave opportunity for that deep and clear analysis, that mighty grasp of
principle, which so much distinguished his higher efforts. His very
statement was argument ; his inference seemed demonstration. The
earnestness of his own conviction wrought conviction in others. One
was convinced, and believed, and assented, because it was gratifying,
delightful, to think, and feel, and believe, in unison with an intellect of
such evident superiority.

Mr. Dexter, sir, such as I have described him, argued the New England cause. He put into his effort his whole heart, as well as all the
powers of his understanding ; for he had avowed, in the most public
manner, his entire concurrence with his neighbors, on the point in dispute. He argued the cause ; it was lost, and New England submitted.
The established tribunals pronounced the law constitutional, and New
England acquiesced. Now, sir, is not this the exact opposite of the
doctrine of the gentleman from South Carolina? According to him,
instead of referring to the judicial tribunals, we should have broken up
the embargo, by laws of our own ; we should have repealed it, *quoad*
New England ; for we had a strong, palpable, and oppressive case. Sir,
we believed the embargo unconstitutional ; but still, that was matter of
opinion, and who was to decide it? We thought it a clear case ; but,
nevertheless, we did not take the laws into our hands, *because we did not
wish to bring about a revolution, nor to break up the Union ;* for I maintain, that, between submission to the decision of the constituted tribunals, and revolution, or disunion, there is no middle ground — there is no
ambiguous condition, half allegiance and half rebellion. There is no
treason, *madcosy.* And, sir, how futile, how very futile it is, to admit the
right of state interference, and then to attempt to save it from the character of unlawful resistance, by adding terms of qualification to the
causes and occasions, leaving all the qualifications, like the case itself, in
the discretion of the state governments. It must be a clear case, it is
said ; a deliberate case ; a palpable case ; a dangerous case. But, then,
the state is still left at liberty to decide for herself what is clear, what is
deliberate, what is palpable, what is dangerous.

Do adjectives and epithets avail any thing? Sir, the human mind is
so constituted, that the merits of both sides of a controversy appear very
clear, and very palpable, to those who respectively espouse them, and
both sides usually grow clearer, as the controversy advances. South
Carolina sees unconstitutionality in the tariff — she sees oppression there,
also, and she sees danger. Pennsylvania, with a vision not less sharp,
looks at the same tariff, and sees no such thing in it — she sees it all constitutional, all useful, all safe. The faith of South Carolina is strengthened by opposition, and she now not only sees, but *resolves*, that the tariff
is palpably unconstitutional, oppressive, and dangerous : but Pennsylvania, not to be behind her neighbors, and equally willing to strengthen her
own faith by a confident asseveration, *resolves* also, and gives to every

warm affirmative of South Caralina, a plain, downright Pennsylvania negative. South Carolina, to show the strength and unity of her opinions, brings her assembly to a unanimity, within seven votes; Pennsylvania, not to be outdone in this respect more than others, reduces her dissentient fraction to five votes. Now, sir, again I ask the gentleman, what is to be done? Are these states both right? Is he bound to consider them both right? If not, which is in the wrong? or, rather, which has the best right to decide?

And if he, and if I, are not to know what the constitution means, and what it is, till those two state legislatures, and the twenty-two others, shall agree in its construction, what have we sworn to, when we have sworn to maintain it? I was forcibly struck, sir, with one reflection, as the gentleman went on with his speech. He quoted Mr. Madison's resolutions to prove that a state may interfere, in a case of deliberate, palpable, and dangerous exercise of a power not granted. The honorable member supposes the tariff law to be such an exercise of power, and that, consequently, a case has arisen in which the state may, if it see fit, interfere by its own law. Now, it so happens, nevertheless, that Mr. Madison himself deems this same tariff law quite constitutional. Instead of a clear and palpable violation, it is, in his judgment, no violation at all. So that, while they use his authority for a hypothetical case, they reject it in the very case before them. All this, sir, shows the inherent futility — I had almost used a stronger word — of conceding this power of interference to the states, and then attempting to secure it from abuse by imposing qualifications of which the states themselves are to judge. One of two things is true: either the laws of the Union are beyond the control of the states, or else we have no constitution of general government, and are thrust back again to the days of the confederacy.

Let me here say, sir, that if the gentleman's doctrine had been received and acted upon in New England, in the times of the embargo and non-intercourse, we should probably not now have been here. The government would very likely have gone to pieces and crumbled into dust. No stronger case can ever arise than existed under those laws; no states can ever entertain a clearer conviction than the New England States then entertained; and if they had been under the influence of that heresy of opinion, as I must call it, which the honorable member espouses, this Union would, in all probability, have been scattered to the four winds. I ask the gentleman, therefore, to apply his principles to that case; I ask him to come forth and declare whether, in his opinion, the New England States would have been justified in interfering to break up the embargo system, under the conscientious opinions which they held upon it. Had they a right to annul that law? Does he admit, or deny? If that which is thought palpably unconstitutional in South Carolina justifies that state in arresting the progress of the law, tell me whether that which was thought palpably unconstitutional also in Massachusetts would have justified her in doing the same thing. Sir, I deny the whole doctrine. It has not a foot of ground in the constitution to stand on. No public man of reputation ever advanced it in Massachusetts, in the warmest times, or could maintain himself upon it there at any time.

I wish now, sir, to make a remark upon the Virginia resolutions of 1798. I cannot undertake to say how these resolutions were understood by those who passed them. Their language is not a little indefinite. In the case of the exercise, by Congress, of a dangerous power, not granted

to them, the resolutions assert the right, on the part of the state, to interfere, and arrest the progress of the evil. This is susceptible of more than
one interpretation. It may mean no more than that the states may interfere by complaint and remonstrance, or by proposing to the people an
alteration of the federal constitution. This would all be quite unobjection-
able; or it may be that no more is meant than to assert the general right
of revolution, as against all governments, in cases of intolerable oppression. This no one doubts; and this, in my opinion, is all that he who
framed these resolutions could have meant by it; for I shall not readily
believe that he was ever of opinion that a state, under the constitution,
and in conformity with it, could, upon the ground of her own opinion of
its unconstitutionality, however clear and palpable she might think the
case, annul a law of Congress, so far as it should operate on herself, by
her own legislative power.

I must now beg to ask, sir, Whence is this supposed right of the states
derived? Where do they get the power to interfere with the laws of the
Union? Sir, the opinion which the honorable gentleman maintains is a
notion founded in a total misapprehension, in my judgment, of the origin
of this government, and of the foundation on which it stands. I hold it
to be a popular government, erected by the people, those who administer
it responsible to the people, and itself capable of being amended and
modified, just as the people may choose it should be. It is as popular,
just as truly emanating from the people, as the state governments. It is
created for one purpose; the state governments for another. It has its
own powers; they have theirs. There is no more authority with them
to arrest the operation of a law of Congress, than with Congress to arrest
the operation of their laws. We are here to administer a constitution
emanating immediately from the people, and trusted by them to our
administration. It is not the creature of the state governments. It is
of no moment to the argument that certain acts of the state legislatures
are necessary to fill our seats in this body. That is not one of their
original state powers, a part of the sovereignty of the state. It is a duty
which the people, by the constitution itself, have imposed on the state
legislatures, and which they might have left to be performed elsewhere,
if they had seen fit. So they have left the choice of president with
electors; but all this does not affect the proposition that this whole government — president, Senate, and House of Representatives — is a popular government. It leaves it still all its popular character. The
governor of a state (in some of the states) is chosen not directly by the
people, but by those who are chosen by the people for the purpose of
performing, among other duties, that of electing a governor. Is the
government of the state on that account not a popular government?
This government, sir, is the independent offspring of the popular will.
It is not the creature of state legislatures; nay, more, if the whole truth
must be told, the people brought it into existence, established it, and have
hitherto supported it, for the very purpose, amongst others, of imposing
certain salutary restraints on state sovereignties. The states cannot now
make war; they cannot contract alliances; they cannot make, each for
itself, separate regulations of commerce; they cannot lay imposts; they
cannot coin money. If this constitution, sir, be the creature of state
legislatures, it must be admitted that it has obtained a strange control
over the volitions of its creators.

The people then, sir, erected this government. They gave it a constitution, and in that constitution they have enumerated the powers which they bestow on it. They have made it a limited government. They have defined its authority. They have restrained it to the exercise of such powers as are granted ; and all others, they declare, are reserved to the states or the people. But, sir, they have not stopped here. If they had, they would have accomplished but half their work. No definition can be so clear as to avoid possibility of doubt ; no limitation so precise as to exclude all uncertainty. Who, then, shall construe this grant of the people ? Who shall interpret their will, where it may be supposed they have left it doubtful ? With whom do they leave this ultimate right of deciding on the powers of the government? Sir, they have settled all this in the fullest manner. They have left it with the government itself, in its appropriate branches. Sir, the very chief end, the main design for which the whole constitution was framed and adopted, was to establish a government that should not be obliged to act through state agency, or depend on state opinion and discretion. The people had had quite enough of that kind of government under the confederacy. Under that system, the legal action — the application of law to individuals — belonged exclusively to the states. Congress could only recommend — their acts were not of binding force till the states had adopted and sanctioned them. Are we in that condition still ? Are we yet at the mercy of state discre tion and state construction ? Sir, if we are, then vain will be our attempt to maintain the constitution under which we sit.

But, sir, the people have wisely provided, in the constitution itself, a proper, suitable mode and tribunal for settling questions of constitutional law. There are, in the constitution, grants of powers to Congress, and restrictions on those powers. There are also prohibitions on the states. Some authority must therefore necessarily exist, having the ultimate juris-diction to fix and ascertain the interpretation of these grants, restrictions, and prohibitions. The constitution has itself pointed out, ordained, and established that authority. How has it accomplished this great and essen-tial end? By declaring, sir, that "*the constitution and the laws of the United States, made in pursuance thereof, shall be the supreme law of the land, any thing in the constitution or laws of any state to the contrary notwithstanding.*"

This, sir, was the first great step. By this, the supremacy of the con-stitution and laws of the United States is declared. The people so will it. No state law is to be valid which comes in conflict with the constitu-tion or any law of the United States. But who shall decide this question of interference ? To whom lies the last appeal ? This, sir, the constitu-tion itself decides also, by declaring "*that the judicial power shall extend to all cases arising under the constitution and laws of the United States.*" These two provisions, sir, cover the whole ground. They are, in truth, the keystone of the arch. With these it is a constitution ; without them it is a confederacy. In pursuance of these clear and express provisions, Congress established, at its very first session, in the judicial act, a mode for carrying them into full effect, and for bringing all questions of consti-tutional power to the final decision of the Supreme Court. It then, sir, became a government. It then had the means of self-protection ; and but for this, it would, in all probability, have been now among things which are passed. Having constituted the government, and declared its powers, the people have further said, that since somebody must decide on the extent of these powers, the government shall itself decide — subject
6

always, like other popular governments, to its responsibility to the people. And now, sir, I repeat, how is it that a state legislature acquires any right to interfere? Who, or what, gives them the right to say to the people, "We, who are your agents and servants for one purpose, will undertake to decide, that your other agents and servants, appointed by you for another purpose, have transcended the authority you gave them"? The reply would be, I think, not impertinent, "Who made you a judge over another's servants? To their own masters they stand or fall."

Sir, I deny this power of state legislatures altogether. It cannot stand the test of examination. Gentlemen may say, that, in an extreme case, a state government might protect the people from intolerable oppression. Sir, in such a case the people might protect themselves, without the aid of the state governments. Such a case warrants revolution. It must make, when it comes, a law for itself. A nullifying act of a state legislature cannot alter the case, nor make resistance any more lawful. In maintaining these sentiments, sir, I am but asserting the rights of the people. I state what they have declared, and insist on their right to declare it. They have chosen to repose this power in the general government, and I think it my duty to support it, like other constitutional powers.

For myself, sir, I doubt the jurisdiction of South Carolina, or any other state, to prescribe my constitutional duty, or to settle, between me and the people, the validity of laws of Congress for which I have voted. I decline her umpirage. I have not sworn to support the constitution according to her construction of its clauses. I have not stipulated, by my oath of office or otherwise, to come under any responsibility, except to the people and those whom they have appointed to pass upon the question, whether the laws, supported by my votes, conform to the constitution of the country. And, sir, if we look to the general nature of the case, could any thing have been more preposterous than to have made a government for the whole Union, and yet left its powers subject, not to one interpretation, but to thirteen or twenty-four interpretations? Instead of one tribunal, established by all, responsible to all, with power to decide for all, shall constitutional questions be left to four and twenty popular bodies, each at liberty to decide for itself, and none bound to respect the decisions of others; and each at liberty, too, to give a new construction, on every new election of its own members? Would any thing, with such a principle in it, or rather with such a destitution of all principle, be fit to be called a government? No, sir. It should not be denominated a constitution. It should be called, rather, a collection of topics for everlasting controversy; heads of debate for a disputatious people. It would not be a government. It would not be adequate to any practical good, nor fit for any country to live under. To avoid all possibility of being misunderstood, allow me to repeat again, in the fullest manner, that I claim no powers for the government by forced or unfair construction. I admit that it is a government of strictly limited powers; of enumerated, specified, and particularized powers; and that whatsoever is not granted is withheld. But, notwithstanding all this, and however the grant of powers may be expressed, its limits and extent may yet, in some cases, admit of doubt; and the general government would be good for nothing, it would be incapable of long existence, if some mode had not been provided in which those doubts, as they should arise, might be peaceably, but authoritatively, solved.

And now, Mr. President, let me run the honorable gentleman's doctrine a little into its practical application. Let us look at his probable *modus operandi.* If a thing can be done, an ingenious man can tell *how* it is to be done. Now, I wish to be informed *how* this state interference is to be put in practice. We will take the existing case of the tariff law. South Carolina is said to have made up her opinion upon it. If we do not repeal it, (as we probably shall not,) she will then apply to the case the remedy of her doctrine. She will, we must suppose, pass a law of her legislature, declaring the several acts of Congress, usually called the tariff laws, null and void, so far as they respect South Carolina, or the citizens thereof. So far, all is a paper transaction, and easy enough. But the collector at Charleston is collecting the duties imposed by these tariff laws — he, therefore, must be stopped. The collector will seize the goods if the tariff duties are not paid. The state authorities will undertake their rescue : the marshal, with his posse, will come to the collector's aid ; and here the contest begins. The militia of the state will be called out to sustain the nullifying act. They will march, sir, under a very gallant leader ; for I believe the honorable member himself commands the militia of that part of the state. He will raise the NULLIFYING ACT on his standard, and spread it out as his banner. It will have a preamble, bearing that the tariff laws are palpable, deliberate, and dangerous violations of the constitution. He will proceed, with his banner flying, to the custom house in Charleston, —

> " all the while
> Sonorous metal blowing martial sounds."

Arrived at the custom house, he will tell the collector that he must collect no more duties under any of the tariff laws. This he will be somewhat puzzled to say, by the way, with a grave countenance, considering what hand South Carolina herself had in that of 1816. But, sir, the collector would, probably, not desist at his bidding. Here would ensue a pause ; for they say, that a certain stillness precedes the tempest. Before this military array should fall on the custom house, collector, clerks, and all, it is very probable some of those composing it would request of their gallant commander-in-chief to be informed a little upon the point of law ; for they have doubtless a just respect for his opinions as a lawyer, as well as for his bravery as a soldier. They know he has read Blackstone and the constitution, as well as Turenne and Vauban. They would ask him, therefore, something concerning their rights in this matter. They would inquire whether it was not somewhat dangerous to resist a law of the United States. What would be the nature of their offence, they would wish to learn, if they, by military force and array, resisted the execution in Carolina of a law of the United States, and it should turn out, after all, that the law *was constitutional.* He would answer, of course, treason. No lawyer could give any other answer. John Fries, he would tell them, had learned that some years ago. How, then, they would ask, do you propose to defend us? We are not afraid of bullets, but treason has a way of taking people off that we do not much relish. How do you propose to defend us? " Look at my floating banner," he would reply ; " see there the *nullifying law!*" Is it your opinion, gallant commander, they would then say, that if we should be indicted for treason, that same floating banner of yours would make a good plea in bar? "South Carolina is a sovereign state," he would reply. That is true ; but would the judge admit our plea? " These tariff laws," he would repeat, " are unconstitutional, palpably, deliberately, dangerously." That all may be so; but if the tribunals should not happen to be of that opinion, shall we swing for it? We are ready to die for our country, but it is rather an awkward business, this dying without touching the ground. After all, this is a sort of *hemp*-tax, worse than any part of the tariff.

Mr. President, the honorable gentleman would be in a dilemma like that of another great general. He would have a knot before him which he could not untie. He must cut it with his sword. He must say to his followers, Defend yourselves with your bayonets; and this is war — civil war.

Direct collision, therefore, between force and force, is the unavoidable result of that remedy for the revision of unconstitutional laws which the gentleman contends for. It must happen in the very first case to which it is applied. Is not this the plain result? To resist, by force, the execution of a law, generally, is treason. Can the courts of the United States take notice of the indulgence of a state to commit treason? The common saying, that a state cannot commit treason herself, is nothing to the purpose. Can it authorize others to do it? If John Fries had produced an act of Pennsylvania, annulling the law of Congress, would it have helped his case? Talk about it as we will, these doctrines go the length of revolution. They are incompatible with any peaceable administration of the government. They lead directly to disunion and civil commotion; and therefore it is, that at the commencement, when they are first found to be maintained by respectable men, and in a tangible form, that I enter my public protest against them all.

The honorable gentleman argues, that if this government be the sole judge of the extent of its own powers, whether that right of judging be in Congress or the Supreme Court, it equally subverts state sovereignty. This the gentleman sees, or thinks he sees, although he cannot perceive how the right of judging, in this matter, if left to the exercise of state legislatures, has any tendency to subvert the government of the Union. The gentleman's opinion may be that the right *ought not* to have been lodged with the general government; he may like better such a constitution as we should have under the right of state interference; but I ask him to meet me on the plain matter of fact — I ask him to meet me on the constitution itself — I ask him if the power is not found there — clearly and visibly found there.

But, sir, what is this danger, and what the grounds of it? Let it be remembered, that the constitution of the United States is not unalterable. It is to continue in its present form no longer than the people who established it shall choose to continue it. If they shall become convinced that they have made an injudicious or inexpedient partition and distribution of power between the state governments and the general government, they can alter that distribution at will.

If any thing be found in the national constitution, either by original provision or subsequent interpretation, which ought not to be in it, the people know how to get rid of it. If any construction be established, unacceptable to them, so as to become, practically, a part of the constitution, they will amend it at their own sovereign pleasure. But while the people choose to maintain it as it is, while they are satisfied with it, and refuse to change it, who has given, or who can give, to the state legislatures a right to alter it, either by interference, construction, or otherwise? Gentlemen do not seem to recollect that the people have any power to do any thing for themselves; they imagine there is no safety for them any longer than they are under the close guardianship of the state legislatures. Sir, the people have not trusted their safety, in regard to the general constitution, to these hands. They have required other security, and taken other bonds. They have chosen to trust themselves, first, to the plain words of the instrument, and to such construction as the government itself, in doubtful cases, should put on its own powers, under their oaths of office, and subject to their responsibility to them; just as the people of a state trust their own state governments with a similar power. Secondly, they have reposed their trust in the efficacy of frequent elections, and in their own power to remove their own servants and agents, whenever they see cause. Thirdly, they have reposed trust in the judicial power, which, in order that it might be trustworthy, they have made as respectable, as disinterested, and as independent as practicable. Fourthly, they have seen fit to rely, in case of necessity, or high expediency, on their known and admitted power to alter or amend the constitution, peaceably and quietly, whenever experience shall point out defects or imperfections. And finally, the people of the United States have at no time, in no way, directly or indirectly, authorized any state legislature to construe or interpret *their* instrument of government; much less to interfere, by their own power, to arrest its course and operation.

If, sir, the people, in these respects, had done otherwise than they have done, their constitution could neither have been preserved, nor would it have been worth preserving. And if its plain provision shall now be disregarded, and these new doctrines interpolated in it, it will become as feeble and helpless a being as enemies, whether early or more recent, could possibly desire. It will exist in every state, but as a poor dependant on state permission. It must borrow leave to be, and will be, no longer than state pleasure, or state discretion, sees fit to grant the indulgence, and to prolong its poor existence.

But, sir, although there are fears, there are hopes also. The people have preserved this, their own chosen constitution, for forty years, and have seen their happiness, prosperity, and renown grow with its growth and strengthen with its strength. They are now, generally, strongly attached to it. Overthrown by direct assault it cannot be; evaded, undermined, NULLIFIED, it will not be, if we, and those who shall succeed us here, as agents and representatives of the people, shall conscientiously and vigilantly discharge the two great branches of our public trust — faithfully to preserve and wisely to administer it.

Mr. President, I have thus stated the reasons of my dissent to the doctrines which have been advanced and maintained. I am conscious of having detained you, and the Senate, much too long. I was drawn into the debate, with no previous deliberation such as is suited to the discussion of so grave and important a subject. But it a subject of which my heart is full, and I have not been willing to suppress the utterance of its spontaneous sentiments.

I cannot, even now, persuade myself to relinquish it, without expressing, once more, my deep conviction, that since it respects nothing less than the union of the states, it is of most vital and essential importance to the public happiness. I profess, sir, in my career hitherto, to have kept steadily in view the prosperity and honor of the whole country, and the preservation of our Federal Union. It is to that Union we owe our safety at home, and our consideration and dignity abroad. It is to that Union that we are chiefly indebted for whatever makes us most proud of our country. That Union we reached only by the discipline of our virtues in the severe school of adversity. It had its origin in the necessities of disordered finance, prostrate commerce, and ruined credit. Under its benign influences, these great interests immediately awoke, as from the dead, and sprang forth with newness of life. Every year of its duration has teemed with fresh proofs of its utility and its blessings ; and although our territory has stretched out wider and wider, and our population spread farther and farther, they have not outrun its protection· or its benefits. It has been to us all a copious fountain of national, social, personal happiness.   I have not allowed myself, sir, to look beyond the Union, to see what might lie hidden in the dark recesses behind. I have not coolly weighed the chances of preserving liberty, when the bonds that unite us together shall be broken asunder. I have not accustomed myself to hang over the precipice of disunion, to see whether, with my short sight, I can fathom the depth of the abyss below ; nor could I regard him as a safe counsellor in the affairs of this government, whose thoughts should be mainly bent on considering, not how the Union should be best preserved, but how tolerable might be the condition of the people when it shall be broken up and destroyed. While the Union lasts, we have high, exciting, gratifying prospects spread out before us, for us and our children. Beyond that I seek not to penetrate the veil. God grant that, in my day at least, that curtain may not rise. God grant that on my vision never may be opened what lies behind. When my eyes shall be turned to behold, for the last time, the sun in heaven, may I not see him shining on the broken and dishonored fragments of a once-glorious Union ; on states dissevered, discordant, belligerent ; on a land rent with civil feuds, or drenched, it may be, in fraternal blood ! Let their last feeble and lingering glance, rather, behold the gorgeous ensign of the republic, now known and honored throughout the earth, still full high advanced, its arms and trophies streaming in their original lustre, not a stripe erased or polluted, nor a single star obscured — bearing for its motto no such miserable interrogatory as, *What is all this worth ?* nor those other words of delusion and folly, *Liberty first, and Union afterwards ;* but every where, spread all over in characters of living light, blazing on all its ample folds, as they float over the sea and over the land, and in every wind under the whole heavens, that other sentiment, dear to every true American heart — Liberty *and* Union, now and forever, one and inseparable !

MR. WEBSTER'S SPEECH.

In the Senate of the United States, March 7, 1850, on the Slavery Compromise.

THE VICE PRESIDENT. The resolutions submitted by the senator from Kentucky were made the special order of the day at 12 o'clock. On this subject the senator from Wisconsin (Mr. Walker) has the floor.

Mr. WALKER. Mr. President, this vast audience has not assembled to hear me; and there is but one man, in my opinion, who can assemble such an audience. They expect to hear him, and I feel it to be my duty, as well as my pleasure, to give the floor therefore to the senator from Massachusetts. I understand it is immaterial to him upon which of these questions he speaks, and therefore I will not move to postpone the special order.

Mr. WEBSTER. I beg to express my obligations to my friend from Wisconsin, (Mr. Walker,) as well as to my friend from New York, (Mr. Seward,) for their courtesy in allowing me to address the Senate this morning.

Mr. President: I wish to speak to-day, not as a Massachusetts man, nor as a northern man, but as an American, and a member of the Senate of the United States. It is fortunate that there is a Senate of the United States; a body not yet moved from its propriety, not lost to a just sense of its own dignity, and its own high responsibilities, and a body to which the country looks with confidence for wise, moderate, patriotic, and healing counsels. It is not to be denied that we live in the midst of strong agitations, and are surrounded by very considerable dangers to our institutions of government. The imprisoned winds are let loose. The east, the west, the north, and the stormy south, all combine to throw the whole ocean into commotion, to toss its billows to the skies, and to disclose its profoundest depths. I do not affect to regard myself, Mr. President, as holding, or as fit to hold, the helm in this combat of the political elements; but I have a duty to perform, and I mean to perform it with fidelity — not without a sense of surrounding dangers, but not without hope. I have a part to act, net for my own security or safety, for I am looking out for no fragment upon which to float away from the wreck, if wreck there must be, but for the good of the whole, and the preservation of the whole; and there is that which will keep me to my duty during this struggle, whether the sun and the stars shall appear, or shall not appear, for many days. I speak to-day for the preservation of the Union. "Hear me for my cause." I speak to-day, out of a solicitous and anxious heart, for the restoration to the country of that quiet and that harmony which make the blessings of this Union so rich and so dear to us all. These are the topics that I propose to myself to discuss; these are the motives, and the sole motives, that influence me in the wish to communicate my opinions to the Senate and the country; and if I can do any thing, however little, for the promotion of these ends, I shall have accomplished all that I desire.

Mr. President, it may not be amiss to recur very briefly to the events which, equally sudden and extraordinary, have brought the political condition of the country to what it now is. In May, 1846, the United States declared war against Mexico. Her armies, then on the frontiers, entered the provinces of that republic; met and defeated all her troops; penetrated her mountain passes, and occupied her capital. The marine force of the United States took possession of her forts and her towns on the Atlantic and on the Pacific. In less than two years a treaty was negotiated, by which Mexico ceded to the United States a vast territory, extending seven or eight hundred miles along the shores of the Pacific; reaching back over the mountains, and across the desert, and until it joined the frontier of the state of Texas. It so happened that in the distracted and feeble state of the Mexican government, before the declaration of war by the United States against Mexico had become known in California, the people of California, under the lead of American officers, overthrew the existing provincial government of California — the Mexican authorities — and run up an independent flag. When the news arrived at San Francisco that war had been declared by the United States against Mexico, this independent flag was pulled down, and the stars and stripes of this Union hoisted in its stead. So, sir, before the war was over, the powers of the United States, military and naval, had possession of San Francisco and Upper California, and a great rush of emigrants from various parts of the world took place into California in 1846 and 1847. But now, behold another wonder.

In January of 1848, the Mormons, it is said, or some of them, made a discovery of an extraordinary rich mine of gold — or, rather, of a very great quantity of gold, hardly fit to be called a mine, for it was spread near the surface — on the lower part of the South or American branch of the Sacramento. They seem to have attempted to conceal their discovery for some time; but soon another discovery, perhaps of greater importance, was made of gold, in another part of the American branch of the Sacramento, and near Sutter's Fort, as it is called. The fame of these discoveries spread far and wide. They excited more and more the spirit of emigration towards California, which had already been excited; and persons crowded in hundreds, and flocked towards the Bay of San Francisco. This, as I have said, took place in the winter and spring of 1848. The digging commenced in the spring of that year, and from that time to this the work of searching for gold has been prosecuted with a success not heretofore known in the history of this globe. We all know, sir, how incredulous the American public was at the accounts which reached us at first of these discoveries; but we all know now that these accounts received, and continue to receive, daily confirmation; and down to the present moment I suppose the assurances are as strong, after the experience of these several months, of mines of gold apparently inexhaustible in the regions near San Francisco, in California, as they were at any period of the earlier dates of the accounts. It so happened, sir, that although in the time of peace, it became a very important subject for legislative consideration and legislative decision to provide a proper territorial government for California, yet differences of opinion in the counsels of the government prevented the establishment of any such territorial government for California, at the last session of Congress. Under this state of things, the inhabitants of San Francisco and California — then amounting to a great number of people — in the summer of last year, thought it to be their duty to establish a local government. Under the proclamation of General Riley, the people chose delegates to a convention : that convention met at Monterey. They formed a constitution for the state of California, and it was adopted by the people of California in their primary assemblages. Desirous of immediate connection with the United States, its senators were appointed and representatives chosen, who have come hither, bringing with them the authentic constitution of the state of California ; and they now present themselves, asking, in behalf of their state, that the state may be admitted into this Union as one of the United States. This constitution, sir, contains an express prohibition against slavery or involuntary servitude in the state of California. It is said, and I suppose truly, that of the members who composed that convention, some sixteen were natives, and had been residents of the slaveholding states, about twenty-two were from the non-slaveholding states, and the remaining ten members were either native Californians or old settlers in that country. This prohibition against slavery, it is said, was inserted with entire unanimity.

Mr. HALE. Will the senator give way until order is restored ?

The VICE PRESIDENT. The sergeant-at-arms will see that order is restored, and no more persons admitted to the floor.

Mr. CASS. I trust the scene of the other day will not be repeated. The sergeant-at-arms must display more energy in suppressing this disorder.

Mr. HALE. The noise is outside of the door.

Mr. WEBSTER. And it is this circumstance, sir, the prohibition of slavery by that convention, which has contributed to raise — I do not say it has wholly raised — the dispute as to the propriety of the admission of California into the Union under this constitution. It is not to be denied, Mr. President — nobody thinks of denying — that, whatever reasons were assigned at the commencement of the late war with Mexico, it was prosecuted for the purpose of the acquisition of territory, and under the alleged argument that the cession of territory was the only form in which proper compensation could be made to the United States by Mexico for the various claims and demands which the people of this country had against that government. At any rate, it will be found that President Polk's message, at the commencement of the session of December, 1847, avowed that the war was to be prosecuted until some acquisition of territory was made. And, as the acquisition was to be south of the line of the United States, in warm climates and countries, it was naturally, I suppose, expected by the south, that whatever acquisitions were made in that region would be added to the slaveholding portion of the United States. Events have turned out as was not expected, and that expectation has not been realized ; and therefore some degree of disappointment and surprise has resulted, of course. In other words, it is obvious that the question which has so long harassed the country, and at some times very seriously alarmed the minds of wise and good men, has come upon us for a fresh discussion — the question of slavery in these United States.

Now, sir, I propose — perhaps at the expense of some detail and con-

sequent detention of the Senate — to review, historically, this question of
slavery, which, partly in consequence of its own merits, and partly, perhaps mostly, in the manner it is discussed in one and the other portion of
the country, has been a source of so much alienation and unkind feeling
between the different portions of the Union. We all know, sir, that slavery has existed in the world from time immemorial. There was slavery
in the earliest periods of history, in the Oriental nations. There was
slavery among the Jews; the theocratic government of that people made
no injunction against it. There was slavery among the Greeks, and the
ingenious philosophy of the Greeks found, or sought to find, a justification for it exactly upon the grounds which have been assumed for such a
justification in this country; that is, a natural and original difference
among the races of mankind, the inferiority of the black or colored race
to the white. The Greeks justified their system of slavery upon that
ground precisely. They held the African, and in some parts the Asiatic,
tribes to be inferior to the white race; but they did not show, I think, by
any close process of logic, that, if this were true, the more intelligent and
the stronger had, therefore, a right to subjugate the weaker.

The more manly philosophy and jurisprudence of the Romans placed
the justification of slavery on entirely different grounds.

The Roman jurists, from the first, and down to the fall of the empire,
admitted that slavery was against the natural law, by which, as they maintained, all men, of whatsoever clime, color, or capacity, were equal; but
they justified slavery, first, upon the ground and authority of the law of
nations — arguing, and arguing truly, that at that day the conventional
law of nations admitted that captives in war, whose lives, according to the
notions of the times, were at the absolute disposal of the captors, might,
in exchange for exemption from death, be made slaves for life, and that
such servitude might extend to their posterity. The jurists of Rome
also maintained that, by the civil law, there might be servitude — slavery,
personal and hereditary; first, by the voluntary act of an individual who
might sell himself into slavery; second, by his being received into a state
of slavery by his creditors in satisfaction of a debt; and, thirdly, by
being placed in a state of servitude or slavery for crime. At the introduction of Christianity into the world, the Roman world was full of slaves,
and I suppose there is to be found no injunction against that relation
between man and man in the teachings of the gospel of Jesus Christ, or
of any of his apostles. The object of the instruction imparted to mankind by the Founder of Christianity was to touch the heart, purify the
soul, and improve the lives of individual men. That object went directly
to the first fountain of all political and all social relations of the human
race — the individual heart and mind of man.

Now, sir, upon the general nature, and character, and influence of slavery,
there exists a wide difference between the northern portion of this country and the southern. It is said on the one side that, if not the subject
of any injunction or direct prohibition in the New Testament, slavery is a
wrong; that it is founded merely in the right of the strongest; and that
it is an oppression, like all unjust wars, like all those conflicts by which a
mighty nation subjects a weaker nation to their will; and that slavery, in
its nature, whatever may be said of it in the modifications which have
taken place, is not, in fact, according to the meek spirit of the gospel. It
is not kindly affectioned; it does not " seek another's, and not its own." It
does not " let the oppressed go free." These are sentiments that are

cherished, and recently with greatly augmented force, among the people of the Northern States. It has taken hold of the religious sentiment of that part of the country, as it has more or less taken hold of the religious feelings of a considerable portion of mankind. The south, upon the other side, having been accustomed to this relation between the two races all their lives, from their birth — having been taught in general to treat the subjects of this bondage with care and kindness — and I believe, in general, feeling for them great care and kindness — have yet not taken this view of the subject which I have mentioned. There are thousands of religious men, with consciences as tender as any of their brethren at the north, who do not see the unlawfulnesss of slavery; and there are more thousands, perhaps, that, whatsoever they may think of it in its origin, and as a matter depending upon natural right, yet take things as they are, and, finding slavery to be an established relation of the society in which they live, can see no way in which — let their opinions on the abstract question be what they may — it is in the power of the present generation to relieve themselves from this relation. And in this respect candor obliges me to say, that I believe they are just as conscientious, many of them, and of the religious people all of them, as they are in the north in holding different opinions.

Why, sir, the honorable senator from South Carolina, the other day, alluded to the separation of that great religious community, the Methodist Episcopal Church. That separation was brought about by differences of opinion upon this peculiar subject of slavery. I felt great concern, as that dispute went on, about the result, and I was in hopes that the difference of opinion might be adjusted, because I looked upon that religious denomination as one of the great props of religion and morals throughout the whole country, from Maine to Georgia. The result was against my wishes and against my hopes. I have read all their proceedings, and all their arguments, but I have never yet been able to come to the conclusion that there was any real ground for that separation; in other words, that no good could be produced by that separation. I must say I think there was some want of candor and charity. Sir, when a question of this kind takes hold of the religious sentiments of mankind, and comes to be discussed in religious assemblies of the clergy and laity, there is always to be expected, or always to be feared, a great degree of excitement. It is in the nature of man, manifested by his whole history, that religious disputes are apt to become warm, and men's strength of conviction is proportionate to their views of the magnitude of the questions. In all such disputes there will sometimes men be found with whom every thing is absolute — absolutely wrong, or absolutely right. They see the right clearly; they think others ought so to see it, and they are disposed to establish a broad line of distinction between what is right and what is wrong. And they are not seldom willing to establish that line upon their own convictions of the truth and the justice of their own opinions; and are willing to mark and guard that line, by placing along it a series of dogmas, as lines of boundary are marked by posts and stones. There are men who, with clear perceptions, as they think, of their own duty, do not see how too hot a pursuit of one duty may involve them in the violation of others, or how too warm an embracement of one truth may lead to a disregard of other truths equally important. As I heard it stated strongly, not many days ago, these persons are disposed to mount upon some particular duty as

upon a war horse, and to drive furiously, on, and upon, and over all other
duties that may stand in the way. There are men who, in times of that
sort, and disputes of that sort, are of opinion that human duties may be
ascertained with the exactness of mathematics. They deal with morals
as with mathematics, and they think what is right may be distinguished
from what is wrong with the precision of an algebraic equation. They
have, therefore, none too much charity towards others who differ from
them. They are apt, too, to think that nothing is good but what is perfect, and that there are no compromises or modifications to be made in
submission to difference of opinion, or in deference to other men's judgment. If their perspicacious vision enables them to detect a spot on the
face of the sun, they think that a good reason why the sun should
be struck down from heaven. They prefer the chance of running
into utter darkness, to living in heavenly light, if that heavenly light be
not absolutely without any imperfection. There are impatient men —
too impatient always to give heed to the admonition of St. Paul, "that we
are not to do evil that good may come" — too impatient to wait for the
slow progress of moral causes, in the improvement of mankind. They
do not remember, that the doctrines and the miracles of Jesus Christ
have, in eighteen hundred years, converted only a small portion of the
human race; and among the nations that are converted to Christianity,
they forget how many vices and crimes, public and private, still prevail,
and that many of them — public crimes especially, which are offences
against the Christian religion — pass without exciting particular regret or
indignation. Thus wars are waged, and unjust wars. I do not deny
that there may be just wars. There certainly are; but it was the remark
of an eminent person, not many years ago, on the other side of the Atlantic, that it was one of the greatest reproaches to human nature that
wars were sometimes necessary. The defence of nations sometimes
causes a war against the injustice of other nations.

Now, sir, in this state of sentiment upon the general nature of slavery,
lies the cause of a great portion of those unhappy divisions, exaspera-
tions, and reproaches which find vent and support in different parts of the
Union. Slavery does exist in the United States. It did exist in the
states before the adoption of this constitution, and at that time.

And now let us consider, sir, for a moment, what was the state of sentiment, north and south, in regard to slavery, at the time this constitution
was adopted. A remarkable change has taken place since; but what did
the wise and great men of all parts of the country think of slavery? — in
what estimation did they hold it then, when this constitution was adopted?
Now, it will be found, sir, if we will carry ourselves by historical research
back to that day, and ascertain men's opinions by authentic records still
existing among us, that there was no great diversity of opinion between
the north and the south upon the subject of slavery; and it will be
found that both parts of the country held it equally an evil — a moral and
political evil. It will not be found that either at the north or at the
south there was much, though there was some, invective against slavery,
as inhuman and cruel. The great ground of objection to it was political;
that it weakened the social fabric; that, taking the place of free labor,
society was less strong and labor was less productive; and, therefore, we
find, from all the eminent men of the time, the clearest expression of
their opinion that slavery was an evil. And they ascribed its existence

here, not without truth, and not without some acerbity of temper and force of language, to the injurious policy of the mother country, who, to favor the navigator, had entailed these evils upon the colonies. I need hardly refer, sir, to the publications of the day. They are matters of history on the record. The eminent men, the most eminent men, and nearly all the conspicuous politicians of the south, held the same sentiments; that slavery was an evil, a blight, a blast, a mildew, a scourge, and a curse. There are no terms of reprobation of slavery so vehement in the north of that day as in the south. The north was not so much excited against it as the south, and the reason is, I suppose, because there was much less at the north, and the people did not see, or think they saw, the evils so prominently as they were seen, or thought to be seen, at the south.

Then, sir, when this constitution was framed, this was the light in which the convention viewed it. The convention reflected the judgment and sentiments of the great men of the south. A member of the other house, whom I have not the honor to know in a recent speech, has collected extracts from these public documents. 'They prove the truth of what I am saying, and the question then was, how to deal with it, and how to deal with it as an evil. Well, they came to this general result. They thought that slavery could not be continued in the country, if the importation of slaves were made to cease, and therefore they provided that after a certain period the importation might be prevented by the act of the new government. Twenty years were proposed by some gentleman, — a northern gentleman, I think, — and many of the southern gentlemen opposed it as being too long. Mr. Madison especially was something warm against it. He said it would bring too much of this mischief into the country to allow the importation of slaves for such a period. Because we must take along with us, in the whole of this discussion, when we are considering the sentiments and opinions in which this constitutional provision originated, that the conviction of all men was, that, if the importation of slaves ceased, the white race would multiply faster than the black race, and that slavery would therefore gradually wear out and expire. It may not be improper here to allude to that, I had almost said, celebrated opinion of Mr. Madison. You observe, sir, that the term "slave" or "slavery" is not used in the constitution. The constitution does not require that "fugitive slaves" shall be delivered up. It requires that "persons bound to service in one state, and escaping into another, shall be delivered up." Mr. Madison opposed the introduction of the term "slave" or "slavery" into the constitution; for he said that he did not wish to see it recognized by the constitution of the United States of America, that there could be property in men. Now, sir, all this took place at the convention in 1787; but connected with this — concurrent and contemporaneous — is another important transaction not sufficiently attended to. The convention for framing this constitution assembled in Philadelphia in May, and sat until September, 1787. During all that time the Congress of the United States was in session at New York. It was a matter of design, as we know, that the convention should not assemble in the same city where Congress was holding its sessions. Almost all the public men of the country, therefore, of distinction and eminence, were in one or the other of these two assemblies; and I think it happened in some instances that the same gentlemen were members of both. If I mistake not, such was the case of Mr. Rufus King, then a

member of Congress from Massachusetts, and at the same time a member
of the convention to frame the constitution from that state. Now, it was
in the summer of 1787, the very time when the convention in Philadelphia
was framing this constitution, that the Congress in New York was framing
the ordinance of 1787. They passed that ordinance on the 13th of July,
1787, at New York, the very month, perhaps the very day, on which
these questions about the importation of slaves and the character of
slavery were debated in the convention at Philadelphia. And, so far
as we can now learn, there was a perfect concurrence of opinion between
these respective bodies ; and it resulted in this ordinance of 1787, excluding slavery as applied to all the territory over which the Congress of
the United States had jurisdiction, and that was all the territory north-
west of .the Ohio. Three years before, Virginia and other states had
made a cession of that great territory to the United States. And a most
magnificent act it was. I never reflect upon it without a disposition to do
honor and justice — and justice would be the highest honor — to Virginia
for that act of cession of her north-western territory. I will say, sir, it
is one of her fairest claims to the respect and gratitude of the United
States, and that perhaps it is only second to that other claim which
attaches to her — that, from her counsels, and from the intelligence and
patriotism of her leading statesmen, proceeded the first idea put into
practice for the formation of a general constitution of the United States.
Now, sir, the ordinance of 1787 applied thus to the whole territory over
which the Congress of the United States had jurisdiction. It was adopted
nearly three years before the constitution of the United States went into
operation, because the ordinance took effect immediately on its passage ;
while the constitution of the United States, having been framed, was to
be sent to the states to be adopted by their conventions, and then a government had to be organized under it. This ordinance, then, was in
operation and force when the constitution was adopted, and this government put in motion, in April, 1789.

Mr. President, three things are quite clear as historical truths. One
is, that there was an expectation that on the ceasing of the importation
of slaves from Africa, slavery would begin to run out. That was hoped
and expected. Another is, that, as far as there was any power in Congress to prevent the spread of slavery in the United States, that power
was executed in the most absolute manner, and to the fullest extent. An
honorable member whose health does not allow him to be here to-day —

A SENATOR. He is here. (Referring to Mr. Calhoun.)

Mr. WEBSTER. I am very happy to hear that he is ; may he long be
in health and the enjoyment of it to serve his country — said, the other
day, that he considered this ordinance as the first in the series of measures calculated to enfeeble the south, and deprive them of their just
participation in the benefits and privileges of this government. He says
very properly that it was done under the old confederation, and before
this constitution went into effect ; but my present purpose is only to say,
Mr. President, that it was done with the entire and unanimous concurrence of the whole south. Why, there it stands ! The vote of every
state in the Union was unanimous in favor of the ordinance, with the
exception of a single individual vote, and that individual was a northern
man. But, sir, the ordinance abolishing or rather prohibiting slavery
north-west of the Ohio has the hand and seal of every southern member
in Congress. The other and third clear historical 'ruth is, that the

convention meant to leave slavery, in the states, as they found it, entirely under the control of the states.

This was the state of things, sir, and this the state of opinion, under which those very important matters were arranged, and those two important things done; that is, the establishment of the constitution, with a recognition of slavery as it existed in the states, and the establishment of the ordinance, prohibiting, to the full extent of all territory owned by the United States, the introduction of slavery into those territories, and the leaving to the states all power over slavery, in their own limits. And here, sir, we may pause. We may reflect for a moment upon the entire coincidence and concurrence of sentiment between the north and the south upon these questions at the period of the adoption of the constitution. But opinions, sir, have changed — greatly changed — changed north and changed south. Slavery is not regarded in the south now as it was then. I see an honorable member of this body paying me the honor of listening to my remarks; he brings to me, sir, freshly and vividly, the sentiments of his great ancestor, so much distinguished in his day and generation, so worthy to be succeeded by so worthy a grandson, with all the sentiments he expressed in the convention of Philadelphia.

Here we may pause. There was, if not an entire unanimity, a general concurrence of sentiment, running through the whole community, and especially entertained by the eminent men of all portions of the country. But soon a change began at the north and the south, and a severance of opinion showed itself — the north growing much more warm and strong against slavery, and the south growing much more warm and strong in its support. Sir, there is no generation of mankind whose opinions are not subject to be influenced by what appears to them to be their present, emergent, selfish, and exigent interest. I impute to the south no particularly selfish view in the change which has come over her. I impute to her certainly no dishonest view. All that has happened has been natural. It has followed those causes which always influence the human mind and operate upon it. What, then, have been the causes which have created so new a feeling in favor of slavery in the south — which have changed the whole nomenclature of the south on the subject — and from being thought of and described in the terms I have mentioned and will not repeat, it has now become an institution, a cherished institution, in that quarter; no evil, no scourge, but a great religious, social, and moral blessing, as I think I have heard it latterly described? I suppose this, sir, is owing to the sudden uprising and rapid growth of the cotton plantations of the south. So far as any motive of honor, justice, and general judgment could act, it was the cotton interest that gave a new desire to promote slavery, to spread it, and to use its labor. I again say that that was produced by the causes which we must always expect to produce like effects; their whole interest became connected with it. If we look back to the history of the commerce of this country, at the early years of this government, what were our exports? Cotton was hardly, or but to a very limited extent, known. The tables will show that the exports of cotton for the years 1790 and '91 were not more than forty or fifty thousand dollars a year. It has gone on increasing rapidly, until it may now, perhaps, in a season of great product and high prices, amount to a hundred millions of dollars. In the years I have mentioned there was more of wax, more of indigo, more of rice, more of almost every article of export from the south, than of cotton. I think I have heard it said, when

Mr. Jay negotiated the treaty of 1794 with England, he did not know that cotton was exported at all from the United States ; and I have heard it said that, after the treaty which gave to the United States the right to carry their own commodities to England, in their own ships, the custom house in London refused to admit cotton, upon an allegation that it could not be an American production, there being, as they supposed, no cotton raised in America. They would hardly think so now !

Well, sir, we know what followed. The age of cotton became a golden age for our southern brethren. It gratified their desire for improvement and accumulation at the same time that it excited it. The desire grew by what it fed upon, and there soon came to be an eagerness for other territory, a new area, or new areas, for the cultivation of the cotton crop, and measures leading to this result were brought about, rapidly, one after another, under the lead of southern men at the head of the government, they having a majority in both branches to accomplish their ends. The honorable member from Carolina observed that there has been a majority all along in favor of the north. If that be true, sir, the north has acted either very liberally and kindly, or very weakly ; for they never exercised that majority five times in the history of the government. Never. Whether they were outgeneralled, or whether it was owing to other causes, I shall not stop to consider ; but no man acquainted with the history of the country can deny, that the general lead in the politics of the country for three fourths of the period that has elapsed since the adoption of the constitution has been a southern lead. In 1802, in pursuit of the idea of opening a new cotton region, the United States obtained a cession from Georgia of the whole of her western territory, now embracing the rich and growing state of Alabama. In 1803 Louisiana was purchased from France, out of which the states of Louisiana, Arkansas, and Missouri have been framed, as slaveholding states. In 1819 the cession of Florida was made, bringing another cession of slaveholding property and territory Sir, the honorable member from South Carolina thought he saw in certain operations of the government, such as the manner of collecting the revenue and the tendency of those measures to promote emigration into the country, what accounts for the more rapid growth of the north than the south. He thinks that more rapid growth, not the operation of time, but of the system of government established under this constitution. That is a matter of opinion. To a certain extent it may be so ; but it does seem to me that if any operation of the government could be shown in any degree to have promoted the population, and growth, and wealth of the north, it is much more sure that there are sundry important and distinct operations of the government, about which no man can doubt, tending to promote, and which absolutely have promoted, the increase of the slave interest and the slave territory of the south. Allow me to say that it was not time that brought in Louisiana ; it was the act of men. It was not time that brought in Florida ; it was the act of men. And lastly, sir, to complete those acts of men, which have contributed so much to enlarge the area and the sphere of the institution of slavery, Texas, great, and vast, and illimitable Texas, was added to the Union, as a slave state, in 1845 ; and that, sir, pretty much closed the whole chapter, and settled the whole account. That closed the whole chapter — that settled the whole account, because the annexation of Texas, upon the conditions and under the guaranties upon which she was admitted, did not leave an acre of land, capable of being cultivated by slave labor, between this Capitol and the Rio Grande or the Nueces, or whatever is the proper boundary of Texas — not an acre, not one. From that moment, the whole country, from this place to the western boundary of Texas, was fixed, pledged, fastened, decided, to be slave territory forever, by the solemn guaranties of law. And I now say, sir, as the proposition upon which I stand this day, and upon the truth and firmness of which I intend to act until it is overthrown, that there is not at this moment within the United States, or any territory of the United States, a single foot of land, the character of which, in regard to its being freesoil territory or slave territory, is not fixed by some law, and some irrepealable law, beyond the power of the action of this government. Now, is it not so with respect to Texas? Why, it is most manifestly so. The honorable member from South Carolina, at the time of the admission of Texas, held an important post in the executive department of the government; he was secretary of state. Another eminent person of great activity and adroitness in affairs, I mean the late secretary of the treasury, (Mr. Walker,) was a leading member of this body, and took the lead in the business of annexation; and I must say they did their business faithfully and thoroughly; there was no botch left in it. They rounded it off, and made as close joiner work as ever was put together. Resolutions of annexation were brought into Congress fitly joined together — compact, firm, efficient, conclusive upon the great object which they had in view; and those resolutions passed.

Allow me to read the resolution. It is the third clause of the second section of the resolution of the 1st of March, 1845, for the admission of Texas, which applies to this part of the case. That clause reads in these words: —

"New states, of convenient size, not exceeding four in number, in addition to said state of Texas, and having sufficient population, may hereafter, by the consent of said state, be formed out of the territory thereof, which shall be entitled to admission under the provisions of the federal constitution. And such states as may be formed out of that portion of said territory, lying south of 36° 30' north latitude, commonly known as the Missouri compromise line, shall be admitted into the Union with or without slavery, as the people of each state asking admission may desire; and in such state or states as shall be formed out of said territory north of said Missouri compromise line, slavery or involuntary servitude (except for crime) shall be prohibited."

Now, what is here stipulated, enacted, secured? It is, that all Texas south of 36° 30', which is nearly the whole of it, shall be admitted into the Union as a slave state. It was a slave state, and therefore came in as a slave state; and the guaranty is that new states shall be made out of it, and that such states as are formed out of that portion of Texas lying south of 36° 30' may come in as slave states to the number of four, in addition to the state then in existence, and admitted at that time by these resolutions. I know no form of legislation which can strengthen that. I know no mode of recognition that can add a tittle of weight to it. I listened respectfully to the resolutions of my honorable friend from Tennessee, (Mr. Bell.) He proposed to recognize that stipulation with Texas. But any additional recognition would weaken the force of it, because it stands here on the ground of a contract, a thing done for a consideration. It is a law founded on a contract with Texas, and designed to carry that contract into effect. A recognition founded not on any consideration or any contract would not be so strong as it now stands on the face of the resolution. Now, I know no way, I candidly confess, in which

7

this government, acting in good faith, as I trust it always will, can relieve itself from that stipulation and pledge, by any honest course of legislation whatever.   And, therefore, I say again that, so far as Texas is concerned — the whole of Texas south of 36° 30′, which I suppose embraces all the slave territory — there is no land, not an acre, the character of which is not established by law, a law which cannot be repealed without the violation of a contract, and plain disregard of the public faith.

I hope, sir, it is now apparent that my proposition, so far as Texas is concerned, has been maintained; and the provision in this article — and it has been well suggested by my friend from Rhode Island that that part of Texas which lies north of 34° of north latitude may be formed into free states — is dependent, in like manner, upon the consent of Texas, herself a slave state.

Well, now, sir, how came this? How came it that within these walls, where it is said by the honorable member from South Carolina, that the free states have a majority, this resolution of annexation, such as I have described it, found a majority in both houses of Congress? Why, sir, it found that majority by the great addition of northern votes added to the entire southern vote, or at least, nearly the whole of the southern votes. That majority was made up of northern as well as of southern votes. In the House of Representatives it stood, I think, about eighty southern votes for the admission of Texas, and about fifty northern votes for the admission of Texas. In the Senate the vote stood for the admission of Texas, twenty-seven, and twenty-five against it; and of those twenty-seven votes, constituting a majority for the admission of Texas in this body, no less than thirteen of them came from the free states — four of them were from New England. The whole of these thirteen senators from the free states — within a fraction, you see, of one half of all the votes in this body for the admission of Texas, with its immeasurable extent of slave territory — were sent here by the votes of free states.

Sir, there is not so remarkable a chapter in our history of political events, political parties, and political men, as is afforded by this measure for the admission of Texas, with this immense territory, that a bird cannot fly over in a week. [Laughter.] Sir, New England, with some of her votes, supported this measure. Three fourths of the votes of liberty-loving Connecticut went for it in the other house, and one half here. There was one vote for it in Maine, but I am happy to say, not the vote of the honorable member who addressed the Senate the day before yesterday, (Mr. Hamlin,) and who was then a representative from Maine in the other house; but there was a vote or two from Maine — ay, and there was one vote for it from Massachusetts, the gentleman then representing and now living in the district in which the prevalence of freesoil sentiment, for a couple of years or so, has defeated the choice of any member to represent it in Congress. Sir, that body of northern and eastern men who gave those votes at that time, are now seen taking upon themselves, in the nomenclature of politics, the appellation of the Northern Democracy. They undertook to wield the destinies of this empire — if I may call a republic an empire — and their policy was, and they persisted in it, to bring into this country all the territory they could. They did it under pledges, absolute pledges to the slave interest in the case of Texas, and afterwards they lent their aid in bringing in these new conquests. My honorable friend from Georgia, in March, 1847, moved the Senate to declare that the war ought not to be prosecuted for acquisition, for conquest, for the dismemberment of Mexico. The same northern democracy entirely voted against it. He did not get a vote from them. It suited the views, the patriotism, the elevated sentiments of the northern democracy to bring in a world here, among the mountains and valleys of California and New Mexico, or any other part of Mexico, and then quarrel about it ; to bring it in, and then endeavor to put upon it the saving grace of the Wilmot proviso. There were two eminent and highly-respectable gentlemen from the north and east, then leading gentlemen in this Senate: I refer — and I do so with entire respect, for I entertain for both of those gentlemen in general high regard — to Mr. Dix, of New York, and Mr. Niles, of Connecticut, who voted for the admission of Texas. They would not have that vote any other way than as it stood ; and they would not have it as it did stand. I speak of the vote upon the annexation of Texas. Those two gentlemen would have the resolution of annexation just as it is, and they voted for it just as it is, and their eyes were all open to it. My honorable friend, the member who addressed us the other day from South Carolina, was then secretary of state. His correspondence with Mr. Murphy, the chargé d'affaires of the United States in Texas, had been published. That correspondence was all before those gentlemen, and the secretary had the boldness and candor to avow in that correspondence that the great object sought by the annexation of Texas was to strengthen the slave interest of the south. Why, sir, he said, in so many words ——

Mr. CALHOUN. Will the honorable senator permit me to interrupt him for a moment ?

Mr. WEBSTER. Certainly.

Mr. CALHOUN. I am very reluctant to interrupt the honorable gentleman ; but, upon a point of so much importance, I deem it right to put myself *rectus in curia.* I did not put it upon the ground assumed by the senator. I put it upon this ground — that Great Britain had announced to this country, in so many words, that her object was to abolish slavery in Texas, and through Texas to accomplish the abolishment of slavery in the United States and the world. The ground I put it on was, that it would make an exposed frontier ; and, if Great Britain succeeded in her object, it would be impossible that that frontier could be secured against the aggression of the abolitionists ; and that this government was bound, under the guaranties of the constitution, to protect us against such a state of things.

Mr. WEBSTER. That comes, I suppose, sir, to exactly the same thing. It was, that Texas must be obtained for the security of the slave interest of the south.

Mr. CALHOUN. Another view is very distinctly given.

Mr. WEBSTER. That was the object set forth in the correspondence of a worthy gentleman not now living, who preceded the honorable member from South Carolina in that office. There repose on the files of the department of state, as I have occasion to know, strong letters from Mr. Upshur to the United States minister in England, and I believe there are some to the same minister from the honorable senator himself, asserting to this effect the sentiments of this government, that Great Britain was expected not to interfere to take Texas out of the hands of its then existing government, and make it a free country. But my argument, my suggestion, is this — that those gentlemen who composed the northern democracy when Texas was brought into the Union, saw, with all their eyes, that it was brought in as slave country, and brought in for the purpose of being maintained as slave territory to the Greek kalends. I rather think

the honorable gentleman, who was then secretary of state, might, in some
of his correspondence with Mr. Murphy, have suggested that it was not
expedient to say too much about this object, that it might create some
alarm.   At any rate, Mr. Murphy wrote to him, that England was anxious to get rid of the constitution of Texas, because it was a constitution
establishing slavery; and that what the United States had to do was, to
aid the people of Texas in upholding their constitution; but that nothing
should be said that should offend the fanatical men.   But, sir, the honorable member did avow this object, himself, openly, boldly, and manfully;
he did not disguise his conduct, or his motives.

Mr. CALHOUN.   Never, never.

Mr. WEBSTER.   What he means he is very apt to say.

Mr. CALHOUN.   Always, always.

Mr. WEBSTER.   And I honor him for it.   This admission of Texas
was in 1845.   Then, in 1847, *flagrante bello* between the United States
and Mexico, the proposition I have mentioned was brought forward by
my friend from Georgia, and the northern democracy voted straight ahead
against it.   Their remedy was to apply to the acquisitions, after they
should come in, the Wilmot proviso.   What follows?   These two gentlemen, worthy, and honorable, and influential men — and if they had not
been they could not have carried the measure — these two gentlemen,
members of this body, brought in Texas, and by their votes they also
prevented the passage of the resolution of the honorable member from
Georgia, and then they went home and took the lead in the freesoil
party.   And there they stand, sir!   They leave us here, bound in honor
and conscience by the resolutions of annexation — they leave us here to
take the odium of fulfilling the obligations in favor of slavery which they
voted us into, or else the greater odium of violating those obligations,
while they are at home, making rousing and capital speeches for freesoil
and no slavery.   [Laughter.]   And, therefore, I say, sir, that there is
not a chapter in our history, respecting public measures and public men,
more full of what should create surprise, more full of what does create, in
my mind, extreme mortification, than that of the conduct of this northern
democracy.

Mr. President, sometimes, when a man is found in a new relation to
things around him and to other men, he says the world has changed, and
that he has not changed.   I believe, sir, that our self-respect leads us often
to make this declaration in regard to ourselves, when it is not exactly
true.   An individual is more apt to change, perhaps, than all the world
around him.   But, under the present circumstances, and under the responsibility which I know I incur by what I am now stating here, I feel
at liberty to recur to the various expressions and statements, made at
various times, of my own opinions and resolutions respecting the admission
of Texas, and all that has followed.   Sir, as early as 1836, or in the
earlier part of 1837, a matter of conversation and correspondence between
myself and some private friends was this project of annexing Texas to the
United States; and an honorable gentleman with whom I have had a long
acquaintance, a friend of mine, now perhaps in this chamber — I mean
General Hamilton, of South Carolina — was knowing to that correspondence.   I had voted for the recognition of Texan independence, because I
believed it was an existing fact, surprising and astonishing as it was, and
I wished well to the new republic: but I manifested from the first utter
opposition to bringing her, with her territory, into the Union.   I had

occasion, sir, in 1837, to meet friends in New York, on some political occasion, and I then stated my sentiments upon the subject. It was the first time that I had occasion to advert to it; and I will ask a friend near me to do me the favor to read an extract from the speech, for the Senate may find it rather tedious to listen to the whole of it. It was delivered in Niblo's Garden in 1837.

Mr. GREENE then read the following extract from the speech of the honorable senator, to which he referred: —

" Gentlemen, we all see that, by whomsoever possessed, Texas is likely to be a slaveholding country; and I frankly avow my entire unwillingness to do any thing which shall extend the slavery of the African race on this continent, or add other slaveholding states to the Union.

" When I say that I regard slavery in itself as a great moral, social, and political evil, I only use language which has been adopted by distinguished men, themselves citizens of slaveholding states.

" I shall do nothing, therefore, to favor or encourage its further extension. We have slavery already among us. The constitution found it among us; it recognized it, and gave it solemn guaranties.

" To the full extent of these guaranties we are all bound in honor, in justice, and by the constitution. All the stipulations contained in the constitution in favor of the slaveholding states, which are already in the Union, ought to be fulfilled, and, so far as depends on me, shall be fulfilled in the fulness of their spirit and to the exactness of their letter. Slavery, as it exists in the states, is beyond the reach of Congress. It is a concern of the states themselves. They have never submitted it to Congress, and Congress has no rightful power over it.

" I shall concur, therefore, in no act, no measure, no menace, no indication of purpose which shall interfere or threaten to interfere with the exclusive authority of the several states over the subject of slavery, as it exists within their respective limits. All this appears to me to be matter of plain and imperative duty.

" But when we come to speak of admitting new states, the subject assumes an entirely different aspect. Our rights and our duties are then both different. . . . . .

" I see, therefore, no political necessity for the annexation of Texas to the Union — no advantages to be derived from it; and objections to it of a strong, and, in my judgment, of a decisive character."

Mr. WEBSTER. I have nothing, sir, to add to, nor to take back from, those sentiments. That, the Senate will perceive, was in 1837. The purpose of immediately annexing Texas at that time was abandoned or postponed; and it was not revived with any vigor for some years. In the mean time it had so happened that I had become a member of the executive administration, and was for a short period in the department of state. The annexation of Texas was a subject of conversation — not confidential — with the president and heads of department, as well as with other public men. No serious attempt was then made, however, to bring it about. I left the department of state in May, 1843, and shortly after I learned, though no way connected with official information, that a design had been taken up of bringing in Texas, with her slave territory and population, into the United States. I was here in Washington at the time, and persons are now here who will remember that we had an arranged meeting for conversation upon it. I went home to Massachusetts, and proclaimed the existence of that purpose; but I could get no audience, and but little attention. Some did not believe it, and some were to o much engaged in their own pursuits to give it any heed. They had gone to their farms or to their merchandise, and it was impossible to arouse any sentiment in New England or in Massachusetts that should combine the two great political parties against this annexation ; and, indeed, there was no hope of bringing the northern democracy into that view, for the leaning was all the other way. But, sir, even with whigs, and leading whigs, I am ashamed to say, there was a great indifference towards the admission of Texas with slave territory into this Union. It went on. I was then out of Congress. The annexation resolutions passed the 1st of March, 1845. The legislature of Texas complied with the conditions, and accepted the guaranties ; for the phraseology of the language of the resolution is, that Texas is to come in "upon the conditions and under the guaranties herein prescribed." I happened to be returned to the Senate in March, 1845, and was here in December, 1845, when the acceptance by Texas of the conditions proposed by Congress was laid before us by the president, and an act for the consummation of the connection was laid before the two houses. The connection was not completed. A final law doing the deed of annexation ultimately and finally had not been passed ; and when it was upon its final passage here, I expressed my opposition to it, and recorded my vote in the negative ; and there the vote stands, with the observations that I made upon that occasion. It has happened that between 1837 and this time, on various occasions and opportunities, I have expressed my entire opposition to the admission of slave states, or the acquisition of new slave territories, to be added to the United States. I know, sir, no change in my own sentiments or my own purposes in that respect. I will now again ask my friend from Rhode Island to read another extract from a speech of mine, made at a whig convention in Springfield, Massachusetts, in the month of September, 1847.

Mr. GREENE here read the following extract : —

" We hear much just now of a *panacea* for the dangers and evils of slavery and slave annexation, which they call the '*Wilmot Proviso*.' That certainly is a just sentiment, but it is not a sentiment to found any new party upon. It is not a sentiment on which Massachusetts whigs differ. There is not a man in this hall who holds to it more firmly than I do, nor one who adheres to it more than another.

" I feel some little interest in this matter, sir. Did not I commit myself in 1838 to the whole doctrine, fully, entirely ? And I must be permitted to say that I cannot quite consent that more recent discoveries should claim the merit and take out a patent.

" I deny the priority of their invention. Allow me to say, sir, it is not their thunder.   . . . .

" We are to use the first and last, and every occasion which offers to oppose the extension of slave power.

" But I speak of it here, as in Congress, as a political question, a question for statesmen to act upon. We must so regard it. I certainly do not mean to say that it is less important in a moral point of view, that it is not more important in many other points of view ; but, as a legislator, or in any official capacity, I must look at it, consider it, and decide it as a matter of political action."

Mr. WEBSTER. On other occasions, in debates here, I have expressed my determination to vote for no acquisition, or cession, or annexation, north or south, east or west. My opinion has been, that we have territory enough, and that we should follow the Spartan maxim, "Improve, adorn what you have, seek no farther." I think that it was in some observations that I made here on the three million loan bill, that I avowed that sentiment. In short, sir, the sentiment has been avowed quite as often, in as many places, and before as many assemblies, as any humble sentiments of mine ought to be avowed.

But now that, under certain conditions, Texas is in, with all her territories, as a slave state, with a solemn pledge that if she is divided into many states, those states may come in as slave states south of 36° 30′, how are we to deal with this subject? I know no way of honorable legislation, when the proper time comes for the enactment, but to carry into effect all that we have stipulated to do. I do not entirely agree with my honorable friend from Tennessee, (Mr. Bell,) that, as soon as the time comes when she is entitled to another representative, we should create a new state. The rule in regard to it I take to be this: that, when we have created new states out of territories, we have generally gone upon the idea that when there is population enough to form a state, sixty thousand, or some such thing, we would create a state; but it is quite a different thing when a state is divided, and two or more states made out of it. It does not follow, in such a case, that the same rule of apportionment should be applied. That, however, is a matter for the consideration of Congress, when the proper time arrives. I may not then be here. I may have no vote to give on the occasion; but I wish it to be distinctly understood to-day, that, according to my view of the matter, this government is solemnly pledged by law to create new states out of Texas, with her consent, when her population shall justify such a proceeding; and, so far as such states are formed out of Texan territory lying south of 36° 30′, to let them come in as slave states. That is the meaning of the resolution which our friends, the northern democracy, have left us to fulfil; and I, for one, mean to fulfil it, because I will not violate the faith of the government.

Now, as to California and New Mexico, I hold slavery to be excluded from those territories by a law even superior to that which admits and sanctions it in Texas. I mean the law of nature, — of physical geography, — the law of the formation of the earth. That law settles forever, with a strength beyond all terms of human enactment, that slavery cannot exist in California or New Mexico. Understand me, sir; I mean slavery as we regard it; slaves in gross, of the colored race, transferable by sale and delivery like other property. I shall not discuss this point, but I leave it to the learned gentlemen who have undertaken to discuss it; but I suppose there is no slave of that description in California now. I understand that *peonism*, a sort of penal servitude, exists there, or rather a sort of voluntary sale of a man and his offspring for debt, as it is arranged and exists in some parts of California and New Mexico. But what I mean to say is, that African slavery, as we see it among us, is as utterly impossible to find itself, or to be found, in Mexico, as any other natural impossibility. California and New Mexico are Asiatic in their formation and scenery. They are composed of vast ridges of mountains of enormous height, with broken ridges and deep valleys. The sides of these mountains are barren, entirely barren, their tops capped by perennial snow. There may be in California, now made free by its constitution, and no doubt there are, some tracts of valuable land. But it is not so in New Mexico. Pray, what is the evidence which every gentleman must have obtained on this subject, from information sought by himself or communicated by others? I have inquired and read all I could find in order to obtain information. What is there in New Mexico that could by any possibility induce any body to go there with slaves? There are some narrow strips of tillable land on the borders of the rivers; but the rivers themselves dry up before midsummer is gone. All that the people can do is to raise some little articles, some little wheat for their tortillas, and all that by irrigation. And who expects to see a hundred black men cultivating tobacco, corn, cotton, rice, or any thing else, on lands in New Mexico made fertile only by irrigation? I look upon it, therefore, as a fixed fact, — to use an expression current at this day, — that both California and New Mexico are destined to be free, so far as they are settled at all, which I believe, especially in regard to New Mexico, will be very little for a great length of time; free by the arrangement of things by the Power above us. I have, therefore, to say, in this respect also, that this country is fixed for freedom, to as many persons as shall ever live there, by as irrepealable and more irrepealable a law than the law that attaches to the right of holding slaves in Texas; and I will say further, that if a resolution or a law were now before us to provide a territorial government for New Mexico, I would not vote to put any prohibition into it whatever. The use of such a prohibition would be idle, as it respects any effect it would have upon the territory; and I would not take pains to reaffirm an ordinance of Nature, nor to reenact the will of God. And I would put in no Wilmot proviso for the purpose of a taunt or a reproach. I would put into it no evidence of the votes of superior power, to wound the pride, even whether a just pride, a rational pride, or an irrational pride — to wound the pride of the gentlemen who belong to the Southern States. I have no such object, no such purpose. They would think it a taunt, an indignity; they would think it to be an act taking away from them what they regard a proper equality of privilege; and whether they expect to realize any benefit from it or not, they would think it a theoretic wrong; that something more or less derogatory to their character and their rights had taken place. I propose to inflict no such wound upon any body, unless something essentially important to the country, and efficient to the preservation of liberty and freedom, is to be effected. Therefore, I repeat, sir, and I repeat it because I wish it to be understood, that I do not propose to address the Senate often on this subject. I desire to pour out all my heart in as plain a manner as possible; and I say, again, that if a proposition were now here for a government for New Mexico, and it was moved to insert a provision for a prohibition of slavery, I would not vote for it.

Now, Mr. President, I have established, so far as I proposed to go into any line of observation to establish, the proposition with which I set out, and upon which I propose to stand or fall; and that is, that the whole territory of the states in the United States, or in the newly-acquired territory of the United States, has a fixed and settled character, now fixed and settled by law, which cannot be repealed in the case of Texas without a violation of public faith, and cannot be repealed by any human power in regard to California or New Mexico; that, under one or other of these laws, every foot of territory in the states or in the territories has now received a fixed and decided character.

Sir, if we were now making a government for New Mexico, and any body should propose a Wilmot proviso, I should treat it exactly as Mr. Polk treated that provision for excluding slavery from Oregon. Mr. Polk was known to be in opinion decidedly averse to the Wilmot proviso; but he felt the necessity of establishing a government for the territo. y of Oregon, and though the proviso was there, he knew it would be entirely nugatory; and, since it must be entirely nugatory, since it took away no right, no describable, no estimable, no weighable or tangible right of the south, he said he would sign the bill for the sake of enacting a law to form a government in that territory, and let that entirely useless, and, in that connection, entirely senseless, proviso remain. For myself, I will say that we hear much of the annexation of Canada; and if there be any man, any of the northern democracy, or any one of the freesoil party, who supposes it necessary to insert a Wilmot proviso in a territorial government for New Mexico, that man will of course be of opinion that it is necessary to pro tect the everlasting snows of Canada from the foot of slavery by the same overpowering wing of an act of Congress. Sir, wherever there is a particular good to be done, wherever there is a foot of land to be stayed back from becoming slave territory, I am ready to assert the principle of the exclusion of slavery. I am pledged to it from the year 1837; I have been pledged to it again and again; and I will perform those pledges; but I will not do a thing unnecessary, that wounds the feelings of others, or that does disgrace to my own understanding.

Mr. President, in the excited times in which we live, there is found to exist a state of crimination and recrimination between the north and south. There are lists of grievances produced by each; and those grievances, real or supposed, alienate the minds of one portion of the country from the other, exasperate the feelings, subdue the sense of fraternal connection, and patriotic love, and mutual regard. I shall bestow a little attention, sir, upon these various grievances produced on the one side and on the other. I begin with the complaints of the south. I will not answer, further than I have, the general statements of the honorable senator from South Carolina, that the north has grown upon the south in consequence of the manner of administering this government, in the collecting of its revenues, and so forth. These are disputed topics, and I have no inclination to enter into them. But I will state these complaints, especially one complaint of the south, which has, in my opinion, just foundation; and that is, that there has been found at the north, among individuals, and among the legislators of the north, a disinclination to perform, fully, their constitutional duties in regard to the return of persons bound to service, who have escaped into the free states. In that respect, it is my judgment that the south is right, and the north is wrong. Every member of every northern legislature is bound, like every other officer in the country, by oath, to support the constitution of the United States; and this article of the constitution, which says to these states, they shall deliver up fugitives from service, is as binding in honor and conscience as any other article. No man fulfils his duty in any legislature who sets himself to find excuses, evasions, escapes from this constitutional obligation. I have always thought that the constitution addressed itself to the legislatures of the states or to the states themselves. It says that those persons escaping to other states shall be delivered up, and I confess I have always been of the opinion that it was an injunction upon the states themselves. When it is said that a person escaping into another state, and becoming therefore within the jurisdiction of that state, shall be delivered up, it seems to me the import of the passage is, that the state itself, in obedience to the constitution, shall cause him to be delivered up. That is my judgment. I have always entertained that opinion, and I entertain it now. But when the subject, some years ago, was before the Supreme Court of the United States, the majority of the judges held that the power to cause fugitives from service to be delivered up was a power to be exercised under the authority of this government. I do not know, on the whole, that it may not have been a fortunate decision. My habit is to respect the result of judicial deliberations, and the solemnity of judicial decisions. But as it now stands, the business of seeing that these fugitives are delivered up resides in the power of Congress and the national judicature, and my friend at the head of the judiciary committee has a bill on the subject now before the Senate, with some amendments to it, which I propose to support, with all its provisions, to the fullest extent. And I desire to call the attention of all sober-minded men, of all conscientious men, in the north, of all men who are not carried away by any fanatical idea, or by any false idea whatever, to their constitutional obligations. I put it to all the sober and sound minds at the north, as a question of morals and a question of conscience, What right have they, in their legislative capacity, or any other, to endeavor to get round this constitution, to embarrass the free exercise of the rights secured by the constitution to the persons whose slaves escape from them? None at all; none at all. Neither in the forum of conscience, nor before the face of the constitution, are they justified, in my opinion. Of course it is a matter for their consideration. They probably, in the turmoil of the times, have not stopped to consider of this; they have followed what seems to be the current of thought and of motives, as the occasion arose, and neglected to investigate fully the real question, and to consider their constitutional obligations; as I am sure, if they did consider, they would fulfil them with alacrity. Therefore I repeat, sir, that there is a ground of complaint against the north, well founded, which ought to be removed, which it is now in the power of the different departments of this government to remove, which calls for the enactment of proper laws authorizing the judicature of this government, in the several states, to do all that is necessary for the recapture of fugitive slaves, and for the restoration of them to those who claim them. Wherever I go, and wherever I speak on this subject, — and when I speak here I desire to speak to the whole north, — I say that the south has been injured in this respect, and has a right to complain; and the north has been too careless of what I think the constitution peremptorily and emphatically enjoins upon it as a duty.

Complaint has been made against certain resolutions that emanate from legislatures at the north, and are sent here to us, not only on the subject of slavery in this District, but sometimes recommending Congress to consider the means of abolishing slavery in the states. I should be very sorry to be called upon to present any resolutions here which could not be referable to any committee or any power in Congress; and therefore I should be very unwilling to receive from Massachusetts instructions to present resolutions expressing any opinion whatever upon slavery as it exists at the present moment in the states, for two reasons: because, first, I do not consider that the legislature of Massachusetts has any thing to do with it; and next, I do not consider that I, as her representative here, have any thing to do with it. Sir, it has become, in my opinion, quite too common; and if the legislatures of the states do not like that opinion, they have a great deal more power to put it down than I have to uphold it. It has become, in my opinion, quite too common a practice for the state legislatures to present resolutions here on all subjects, and to instruct us here on all subjects. There is no public man that requires insdruction more than I do, or who requires information more than I do, or desires it more heartily ; but I do not like to have it come in too imperative a shape. I took notice, with pleasure, of some remarks upon this subject, made the other day in the Senate of Massachusetts, by a young man of talent and character, from whom the best hopes may be entertained. I mean Mr. Hillard. He told the Senate of Massachusetts that he would vote for no instructions whatever to be forwarded to members of Congress, nor for any resolutions to be offered expressive of the sense of Massachusetts as to what their members of Congress ought to do. He said that he saw no propriety in one set of public servants giving instructions and reading lectures to another set of public servants. To their own master all of them must stand or fall, and that master is their constituents. I wish these sentiments could become more common, a great deal more common. I have never entered into the question, and never shall, about the binding force of instructions. I will, however, simply say this : if there be any matter of interest pending in this body, while I am a member of it, in which Massachusetts has an interest of her own not adverse to the general interest of the country, I shall pursue her instructions with gladness of heart, and with all the efficiency which I can bring it. But if the question be one which affects her interest, and at the same time affects ·the interests of all other states, I shall no more regard her political wishes or instructions than I would regard the wishes of a man who might appoint me an arbiter or referee to decide some question of important private right, and who might instruct me to decide in his favor. If ever there was a government upon earth, it is this government; if ever there was a body upon earth, it is this body, which should consider itself as composed by agreement of all, appointed by some, but organized by the general consent of all, sitting here under the solemn obligations of oath and conscience to do that which they think is best for the good of the whole.

Then, sir, there are these abolition societies, of which I am unwilling to speak, but in regard to which I have very clear notions and opinions. I do not think them useful. I think their operations for the last twenty years have produced nothing good or valuable. At the same time, I know thousands of them are honest and good men; perfectly well-meaning men. They have excited feelings — they think they must do something for the cause of liberty, and in their sphere of action they do not see what else they can do, than to contribute to an abolition press or an abolition society, or to pay an abolition lecturer. I do not mean to impute gross motives even to the leaders of these societies, but I am not blind to the consequences. I cannot but see what mischiefs their interference with the south has produced. And is it not plain to every man ? Let any gentleman who doubts of that, recur to the debates in the Virginia House of Delegates in 1832, and he will see with what freedom a proposition made by Mr. Randolph for the gradual abolition of slavery was discussed in that body. Every one spoke of slavery as he thought ; very ignominious and disparaging names and epithets were applied to it. The debates in the House of Delegates on that occasion, I believe, were all published. They were read by every colored man who could read, and if there were any who could not read, those debates were read to them by others. At that time Virginia was not unwilling nor afraid to discuss this question, and to let that part of her population know as much of it as they could learn. That was in 1832. As has been said by the honorable member from Carolina, these abolition societies commenced their course of action in 1835. It is said — I do not know how true it may be — that they sent incendiary publications into the slave states; at any event, they attempted to arouse, and did arouse, a very strong feeling; in other words, they created great agitation in the north against southern slavery. Well, what was the result? The bonds of the slaves were bound more firmly than before; their rivets were more strongly fastened. Public opinion, which in Virginia had begun to be exhibited against slavery, and was opening out for the discussion of the question, drew back and shut itself up in its castle. I wish to know whether any body in Virginia can, now, talk as Mr. Randolph, Governor McDowell, and others talked there, openly, and sent their remarks to the press, in 1832. We all know the fact, and we all know the cause; and every thing that this agitating people have done has been, not to enlarge, but to restrain; not to set free, but to bind faster the slave population of the south. That is my judgment. Sir, as I have said, I know many abolitionists in my own neighborhood, very honest, good people, misled, as I think, by strange enthusiasm; but they wish to do something, and they are called on to contribute, and they do contribute; and it is my firm opinion this day, that within the last twenty years, as much money has been collected and paid to the abolition societies, abolition presses, and abolition lecturers, as would purchase the freedom of every slave man, woman, and child in the state of Maryland, and send them all to Liberia. I have no doubt of it. But I have yet to learn that the benevolence of these abolition societies has at any time taken that particular turn. [Laughter.]

Again, sir, the violence of the press is complained of. The press violent! Why, sir, the press is violent every where. There are outrageous reproaches in the north against the south, and there are reproaches in not much better taste in the south against the north. Sir, the extremists in both parts of this country are violent; they mistake loud and violent talk for eloquence and for reason. They think that he who talks loudest reasons the best. And this we must expect, when the press is free — as it is here, and I trust always will be — for, with all its licentiousness, and all its evil, the entire and absolute freedom of the press is essential to the preservation of government on the basis of a free constitution. Wherever it exists, there will be foolish paragraphs and violent paragraphs in the press, as there are, I am sorry to say, foolish speeches and violent speeches in both houses of Congress. In truth, sir, I must say that, in my opinion, the vernacular tongue of the country has become greatly vitiated, depraved, and corrupted by the style of our congressional debates. [Laughter.] And if it were possible for our debates in Congress to vitiate the principles of the people as much as they have depraved their taste, I should cry out, " God save the Republic! "

Well, in all this I see no solid grievance; no grievance presented by the south, within the redress of the government, but the single one to which I have referred; and that is, the want of a proper regard to the injunction of the constitution for the delivery of fugitive slaves.

There are also complaints of the north against the south. I need not go over them particularly. The first and gravest is, that the north adopted the constitution, recognizing the existence of slavery in the states, and recognizing the right, to a certain extent, of representation of the slaves in Congress, under a state of sentiment and expectation which do not now exist; and that, by events, by circumstances, by the eagerness of the south to acquire territory and extend their slave population, the north finds itself — in regard to the influence of the south and the north, of the free states and the slave states — where it never did expect to find itself when they entered the compact of the constitution. They complain, therefore, that, instead of slavery being regarded as an evil, as it was then — an evil which all hoped would be extinguished gradually — it is now regarded by the south as an institution to be cherished, and preserved, and extended; an institution which the south has already extended to the utmost of her power by the acquisition of new territory Well, then, passing from that, every body in the north reads; and every body reads whatsoever the newspapers contain; and the newspapers — some of them, especially those presses to which I have alluded — are careful to spread about among the people every reproachful sentiment uttered by any southern man bearing at all against the north; every thing that is calculated to exasperate, to alienate; and there are many such things, as every body will admit, from the south or some portion of it, which are spread abroad among the reading people; and they do exasperate, and alienate, and produce a most mischievous effect upon the public mind at the north. Sir, I would not notice things of this sort, appearing in obscure quarters; but one thing has occurred in this debate which struck me very forcibly. An honorable member from Louisiana addressed us the other day on this subject. I suppose there is not a more amiable and worthy gentleman in this chamber — nor a gentleman who would be more slow to give offence to any body, and he did not mean in his remarks to give offence. But what did he say? Why, sir, he took pains to run a contrast between the slaves of the south and the laboring people of the north, giving the preference in all points of condition, and comfort, and happiness, to the slaves of the south. The honorable member, doubtless, did not suppose that he gave any offence, or did any injustice. He was merely expressing his opinion. But does he know how remarks of that sort will be received by the laboring people of the north? Why, who are the laboring people of the north? They are the north. They are the people who cultivate their own farms with their own hands; freeholders, educated men, independent men. Let me say, sir, that five sixths of the whole property of the north is in the hands of the laborers of the north; they cultivate their farms, they educate their children, they provide the means of independence; if they are not freeholders, they earn wages; these wages accumulate, are turned into capital, into new freeholds, and small capitalists are created. That is the case, and such the course of things with us, among the industrious and frugal. And what can these people think, when so respectable and worthy a gentleman as the member from Louisiana undertakes to prove that the absolute ignorance and the abject slavery of the south is more in conformity with the high purposes and destiny of immortal, rational, human beings, than the educated, the independent free laborers of the north? There is a more tangible and irritating cause of grievance at the north. Free blacks are constantly employed in the vessels of the north, generally as cooks or stewards. When the vessel arrives, these free colored men are taken on shore by the police or municipal authority, imprisoned, and kept in prison, till the vessel is again ready to sail. This is not only irritating, but exceedingly inconvenient in practice, and seems altogether impracticable and oppressive. Mr. Hoar's mission, some time ago, to South Carolina, was a well-intended effort to remove this cause of complaint. The north thinks such imprisonments illegal and unconstitutional. As the cases occur constantly and frequently, they think it a great grievance.

Now, sir, so far as any of these grievances have their foundation in matters of law, they can be redressed, and ought to be redressed ; and so far as they have their foundation in matters of opinion, in sentiment, in mutual crimination and recrimination, all that we can do is, to endeavor to allay the agitation, and cultivate a better feeling and more fraternal sentiments between the south and the north.

Mr. President, I should much prefer to have heard from every member on this floor declarations of opinion, that this Union should never be dissolved, than the declarations of opinion, that, in any case, under the pressure of any circumstances, such a dissolution was possible. I hear with pain, and anguish, and distress, the word *secession*, especially when it falls from the lips of those who are eminently patriotic, and known to the country, and known all over the world, for their political services. Secession ! Peaceable secession ! Sir, your eyes and mine are never destined to see that miracle. The dismemberment of this vast country without convulsion ! The breaking up of the fountains of the great deep without ruffling the surface ! Who is so foolish — I beg every body's pardon — as to expect to see any such thing ? Sir, he who sees these states now revolving in harmony around a common centre, expecting to see them quit their places, and fly off, without convulsion, may look, the next hour, to see the heavenly bodies rush from their spheres, and jostle against each other in the realms of space, without producing the crash of the universe. There can be no such thing as a peaceable secession. Peaceable secession is an utter impossibility. Is the great constitution under which we live here, covering this whole country — is it to be thawed and melted away by secession, as the snows on the mountain melt under the influence of a vernal sun — disappear almost unobserved, and die off ? No, sir ! No, sir ! I will not state what might produce the disruption of the states ; but, sir, I see it as plainly as I see the sun in heaven — I see that disruption must produce such a war as I will not describe *in its twofold character !*

Peaceable secession ! peaceable secession ! The concurrent agreement of all the members of this great republic to separate ! A voluntary separation, with alimony on one side and on the other ! Why, what would be the result ? Where is the line to be drawn ? What states are to secede ? What is to remain American ? What am I to be ? An American no longer ? Where is the flag of the republic to remain ? Where is the eagle still to tower ? or is he to cower, and shriek, and fall to the ground ? Why, sir, our ancestors — our fathers and our grandfathers, those of them that are yet living amongst us with prolonged lives — would rebuke and reproach us ; and our children and our grandchildren would cry out shame upon us, if we of this generation should dishonor these ensigns of the power of the government and the harmony of the Union which is every day felt among us with so much joy and gratitude. What is to become of the army ? What is to become of the navy ? What is to become of the public lands ? How is each of the thirty states to defend itself ? I know, although the idea has not been stated distinctly. There is to be a Southern Confederacy. I do not mean, when I allude to this statement, that any one seriously contemplates such a state of things. I do not mean to say that it is true, but I have heard it suggested elsewhere, that that idea has originated in a design to separate. I am sorry, sir, that it has ever been thought of, talked of, or dreamed of, in the wildest flights of human imagination. But the idea must be of a separation including the slave states upon one side, and the free states on the other. Sir, there is not — I may express myself too strongly, perhaps, but some things, some moral things, are almost as impossible as other natural or physical things ; and I hold the idea of a separation of these states, those that are free to form one government, and those that are slaveholding to form another, as a moral impossibility. We could not separate the states by any such line, if we were to draw it. We could not sit down here to-day, and draw a line of separation that would satisfy any five men in the country. There are natural causes that would keep and tie us together ; and there are social and domestic relations which we could not break if we would, and which we should not if we could. Sir, nobody can look over the face of this country at the present moment — nobody can see where its population is the most dense and growing — without being ready to admit, and compelled to admit, that ere long America will be in the valley of the Mississippi.

Well, now, sir, I beg to inquire what the wildest enthusiast has to say on the possibility of cutting off that river, and leaving free states at its source and its branches, and slave states down near its mouth. Pray, sir, pray, sir, let me say to the people of this country, that these things are worthy of their pondering and of their consideration. Here, sir, are five millions of freemen in the free states north of the River Ohio ; can any body suppose that this population can be severed by a line that divides them from the territory of a foreign and an alien government, down somewhere, the Lord knows where, upon the lower banks of the Mississippi? What would become of Missouri? Will she join the arrondissement of the slave states? Shall the man from the Yellow Stone and the Platte River be connected, in the new republic, with the man who lives on the southern extremity of the Cape of Florida? Sir, I am ashamed to pursue this line of remark. I dislike it ; I have an utter disgust for it. I would rather hear of natural blasts and mildews, war, pestilence, and famine, than to hear gentlemen talk of secession. To break up — to break up this great government — to dismember this great country — to astonish Europe with an act of folly such as Europe for two centuries has never beheld in any government ! No, sir ; no, sir ! There will be no secession. Gentlemen are not serious when they talk of secession !

Sir, I hear there is to be a convention held at Nashville. I am bound to believe, that, if worthy gentlemen meet at Nashville in convention, their object will be to adopt counsels conciliatory — to advise the south to forbearance and moderation, and to advise the north to forbearance and moderation, and to inculcate principles of brotherly love and affection, and attachment to the constitution of the country as it now is. I believe, if the convention meet at all, it will be for this purpose ; for certainly, if they meet for any purpose hostile to the Union, they have been singularly inappropriate in their selection of a place. I remember, sir, that when the treaty was concluded between France and England at the peace of Amiens, a stern old Englishman, and an orator, who disliked the terms of the peace as ignominious to England, said in the House of Commons, that, if King William could know the terms of that treaty, he would turn in his coffin. Let me commend the saying of Mr. Windham, in all its emphasis and in all its force, to any persons who shall meet at Nashville for the purpose of concerting measures for the overthrow of the Union of this country over the bones of Andrew Jackson.

Sir, I wish to make two remarks, and hasten to a conclusion. I wish to say, in regard to Texas, that if it should be hereafter at any time the pleasure of the government of Texas to cede to the United States a portion, larger or smaller, of her territory which lies adjacent to New Mexico, and north of 34° of north latitude, to be formed into free states, for a fair equivalent in money, or in the payment of her debt, I think it an object well worthy the consideration of Congress, and I shall be happy to concur in it myself, if I should be in the public councils of the country at the time.

I have one other remark to make. In my observations upon slavery, as it has existed in the country, and as it now exists, I have expressed no opinion of the mode of its extinguishment or amelioration. I will say, however, though I have nothing to propose on that subject, because I do not deem myself competent as other gentlemen to consider it, that if any gentleman from the south shall propose a scheme of colonization, to be carried on by this government, upon a large scale, for the transportation of free colored people to any colony, or any place in the world, I should be quite disposed to incur almost any degree of expense to accomplish that object. Nay, sir, following an example set here more than twenty years ago, by a great man, then a senator from New York, I would return to Virginia — and through her, for the benefit of the whole south — the money received from the lands and territories ceded by her to this government, for any such purpose as to relieve, in whole or in part, or in any way to diminish or deal beneficially with the free colored population of the Southern States. I have said that I honor Virginia for her cession of this territory. There have been received into the treasury of the United States eighty millions of dollars, the proceeds of the sales of public lands ceded by Virginia. If the residue should be sold at the same rate, the whole aggregate will exceed two hundred millions of dollars. If Virginia and the south see fit to adopt any proposition to relieve themselves from the free people of color among them, they have my free consent that the government shall pay them any sum of money out of its proceeds which may be adequate to the purpose.

And now, Mr. President, I draw these observations to a close. I have spoken freely, and I meant to do so. I have sought to make no display ; I have sought to enliven the occasion by no animated discussion ; nor have I attempted any train of elaborate argument. I have sought only to speak my sentiments, fully and at large, being desirous, once and for all, to let the Senate know, and to let the country know, the opinions and sentiments which I entertain on all these subjects. These opinions are not likely to be suddenly changed. If there be any future service that I can render to the country, consistently with these sentiments and opinions, I shall cheerfully render it. If there be not, I shall still be glad to have had an opportunity to disburden my conscience from the bottom of my heart, and to make known every political sentiment that therein exists.

And now, Mr. President, instead of speaking of the possibility or utility of secession, instead of dwelling in these caverns of darkness, instead of groping with those ideas so full of all that is horrid and horrible, let us come out into the light of day ; let us enjoy the fresh airs of Liberty and Union ; let us cherish those hopes which belong to us ; let us devote our-

selves to those great objects that are fit for our consideration and our
action; let us raise our conceptions to the magnitude and the importance
of the duties that devolve upon us; let our comprehension be as broad as
the country for which we act, our aspirations as high as its certain
destiny; let us not be pygmies in a case that calls for men. Never did
there devolve on any generation of men higher trusts than now devolve
upon us for the preservation of this constitution, and the harmony and
peace of all who are destined to live under it. Let us make our generation one of the strongest and the brightest links in that golden chain
which is destined, I fondly believe, to grapple the people of all the states
to this constitution, for ages to come. It is a great popular constitutional
government, guarded by legislation, by law, by judicature, and defended
by the whole affections of the people. No monarchical throne presses
these states together; no iron chain of despotic power encircles them;
they live and stand upon a government popular in its form, representative in its character, founded upon principles of equality, and calculated,
we hope, to last forever. In all its history it has been beneficent: it has
trodden down no man's liberty; it has crushed no state. Its daily respira-
tion is liberty and patriotism, its yet youthful veins all full of enterprise,
courage, and honorable love of glory and renown. Large before, the
country has now, by recent events, become vastly larger. This republic
now extends, with a vast breadth, across the whole continent. The two
great seas of the world wash the one and the other shore. We realize, on
a mighty scale, the beautiful description of the ornamental edging of the
buckler of Achilles: —

> "Now the broad shield complete the artist crowned
> With his last hand, and poured the ocean round;
> In living silver seemed the waves to roll,
> And beat the buckler's verge, and bound the whole."

Mr. CALHOUN. I rise to correct what I conceive to be an error of the
distinguished senator from Massachusetts, as to the motives which induced the acquisition of Florida, Louisiana, and Texas. He attributed
it to the great growth of cotton, and the desire of the southern people to
get an extension of territory, with the view of cultivating it with more
profit than they could in a compact and crowded settlement. Now, Mr.
President, the history of these acquisitions, I think, was not correctly
given. It is well known that the acquisition of Florida was the result of
an Indian war. The Seminole Indians residing along the line attacked
one of our fortresses; troops were ordered out; they were driven back;
and, under the command of General Jackson, Pensacola and St. Marks
were seized. It was these acts, and not the desire for the extended cultivation of cotton, which led to the acquisition of Florida. I admit that
there had been for a long time a desire on the part of the south, and of
the administration, I believe, to acquire Florida; but it was very different
from the reason assigned by the honorable senator. There were collected
together four tribes of Indians — the Creeks, the Choctaws, the Chicka-
saws, and the Cherokees, about thirty thousand warriors — who held connection, almost the whole of them, with the Spanish authorities in Florida,
and carried on a trade perpetually with them. It was well known that a
most pernicious influence was thus exercised over them; and it was the
desire of preventing conflict between the Indians and ourselves in the
south, as I believe, which induced the acquisition of Florida. I come

8

now to Louisiana. We well know that the immediate cause for **the** acquisition of Louisiana was the suspension of our right of deposit at New Orleans. Under a treaty with Spain we had a right to the navigation of the river as far as New Orleans, and a right to make deposits in the port of New Orleans. The Spanish authorities interrupted that right, and that interruption produced a great agitation at the west, and I may say, throughout the whole United States. The gentlemen then in opposition, a highly respectable party — the old federal party, which I have never said a word of disrespect' in regard to — if I mistake not, took the lead in a desire to resort to arms to acquire that territory. Mr. Jefferson, more prudent, desired to procure it by purchase. A purchase was made, in order to remove the difficulty, and to give an outlet to the west to the ocean. That was the immediate cause of the acquisition of Louisiana. Now, sir, we come to Texas. Perhaps no gentleman had more to do with the acquisition of Texas than myself; and I aver, Mr. President, that I would have been among the very last individuals in the United States to have made any movement at that time for the acquisition of Texas; and I go further: if I know myself, I was incapable of acquiring any territory simply on the ground that it was to be an enlargement of slave territory. I would just as freely have acquired it if it had been or the northern as on the southern side. No, sir; very different motives actuated me. I knew at a very early period — I will not go into the history of it — the British government had given encouragement to the abolitionists of the United States, who were represented at the World's Convention. The question of the abolition of slavery was agitated in that convention. One gentleman stated that Mr. Adams informed him that if the British government wished to abolish slavery in the United States, they must begin with Texas. A commission was sent from this World's Convention to the British secretary of state, Lord Aberdeen; and it so happened that a gentleman was present when the interview took place between Lord Aberdeen and the committee, who gave me a full account of it shortly after it occurred. Lord Aberdeen fell into the project, and gave full encouragement to the abolitionists. Well, sir, it is well known that Lord Aberdeen was a very direct, and in my opinion, a very honest and worthy man; and when Mr. Pakenham was sent to negotiate with regard to Oregon, and incidentally with respect to Texas, he was ordered to read a declaration to this government, stating that the British government was anxious to put an end to slavery all over the world, commencing at Texas. It is well known, further, that at that very time a negotiation was going on between France and England to accomplish that object, and our government was thrown by stratagem out of the negotiation; and that object was, first, to induce Mexico to acknowledge the independence of Texas upon the ground that she would abolish it. All these are matters of history; and where is the man so blind — I am sure the senator from Massachusetts is not so blind — as not to see that if the project of Great Britain had been successful, the whole frontier of the states of Louisiana and Arkansas, and the adjacent states, would have been exposed to the inroads of British emissaries. Sir, so far as I was concerned, I put it exclusively upon that ground. I never would run into the folly of reannexation, which I always held to be absurd. Nor, sir, would I put it upon the ground — which I might well have put it — of commercial and manufacturing considerations; because those were not my motive principles, and I chose to assign what were. So far as commerce and manufactures were concerned, I would not have moved in the matter at that early period.

The senator objects that many northern gentlemen voted for annexation. Why, sir, it was natural that they should be desirous of fulfilling the obligations of the constitution; and besides, what man at that time doubted that the Missouri compromise line would be adopted, and that the territory would fall entirely to the south? All that northern men asked for at that time was the extension of that line. Their course, in my opinion, was eminently correct and patriotic.

Now, Mr. President, having made these corrections, I must go back a little farther, and correct a statement which I think the senator has left very defective, relative to the ordinance of 1787. He states, very correctly, that it commenced under the old confederation; that it was afterwards confirmed by Congress; that Congress was sitting in New York at the time, while the convention sat in Philadelphia; and that there was concert of action. I have not looked into the ordinance very recently, but my memory will serve me thus far, that Mr. Jefferson introduced his first proposition to exclude slavery in 1784. There was a vote taken upon it, and I think on that vote every southern senator voted against it; but I am not certain of it. One thing I am certain of, that it was three years before the ordinance could pass. It was sturdily resisted down to 1787; and when it was passed, as I have good reason to believe, it was upon a principle of compromise: first, that the ordinance should contain a provision similar to the one put in the constitution with respect to fugitive slaves; and next, that it should be inserted in the constitution; and this was the compromise upon which the prohibition was inserted in the ordinance of 1787. We thought we had an indemnity in that, but we made a great mistake. Of what possible advantage has it been to us? Violated faith has met us on every side, and the advantage has been altogether in their favor. On the other side, it has been thrown open to a northern population, to the entire exclusion of the southern. This was the leading measure which destroyed the compromise of the constitution, and then followed the Missouri compromise, which was carried mainly by northern votes, although now disavowed and not respected by them. That was the next step, and between these two causes the equilibrium has been broken.

Having made these remarks, let me say that I took great pleasure in listening to the declarations of the honorable senator from Massachusetts upon several points. He puts himself upon the fulfilment of the contract of Congress in the resolutions of Texas annexation, for the admission of the four new states provided for by those resolutions to be formed out of the territory of Texas. All that was manly, statesmanlike, and calculated to do good, because just. He went further; he condemned, and rightfully condemned, and in that he has shown great firmness, the course of the north relative to the stipulations of the constitution for the restoration of fugitive slaves; but permit me to say, for I desire to be candid upon all subjects, that if the senator, together with many friends on this side of the chamber, puts his confidence in the bill which has been reported here, further to extend the laws of Congress upon this subject, it will prove fallacious. It is impossible to execute any law of Congress until the people of the states shall coöperate.

I heard the gentleman with great pleasure say that he would not vote for the Wilmot proviso, for he regarded such an act unnecessary, considering that nature had already excluded slavery. As far as the new acquisitions are concerned, I am disposed to leave them to be disposed of as the hand of nature shall determine. It is what I always have insisted upon. Leave that portion of the country more natural to a non-slaveholding population to be filled by that description of population; and leave that portion into which slavery would naturally go, to be filled by a slaveholding population — destroying artificial lines; though perhaps they may be better than none. Mr. Jefferson spoke like a prophet of the effect of the Missouri compromise line. I am willing to leave it for nature to settle; and to organize governments for the territories, giving all free scope to enter and prepare themselves to participate in their privileges. We want, sir, nothing but justice. When the gentleman says that he is willing to leave it to nature, I understand he is willing to remove all impediments, whether real or imaginary. It is consummate folly to assert that the Mexican law prohibiting slavery in California and New Mexico is in force; and I have always regarded it so.

No man would feel more happy than myself to believe that this Union formed by our ancestors should live forever. Looking back to the long course of forty years' service here, I have the consolation to believe that I have never done one act which would weaken it; that I have done full justice to all sections. And if I have ever been exposed to the imputation of a contrary motive, it is because I have been willing to defend my section from unconstitutional encroachments. But I cannot agree with the senator from Massachusetts that this Union cannot be dissolved. Am I to understand him that no degree of oppression, no outrage, no broken faith, can produce the destruction of this Union? Why, sir, if that becomes a fixed fact, it will itself become the great instrument of producing oppression, outrage, and broken faith. No, sir, the Union can be broken. Great moral causes will break it if they go on, and it can only be preserved by justice, good faith, and a rigid adherence to the constitution.

Mr. WEBSTER. Mr. President, a single word in reply to the honorable member from South Carolina. My distance from the honorable member, and the crowded state of the room, prevented me from hearing the whole of his remarks. I have only one or two observations to make; and, to begin, I first notice the honorable member's last remark. He asks me if I hold the breaking up of the Union by any such thing as the voluntary secession of states as an impossibility. I know, sir, this Union can be broken up; every government can be; and I admit that there may be such a degree of oppression as will warrant resistance and a forcible severance. That is revolution! Of that ultimate right of revolution I have not been speaking. I know that that law of necessity does exist. I forbear from going further, because I do not wish to run into a discussion of the nature of this government. The honorable member and myself have broken lances sufficiently often before on that subject.

Mr. CALHOUN. I have no desire to do it now.

Mr. WEBSTER. I presume the gentleman has not, and I have quite as little. The gentleman refers to the occasions on which these great acquisitions were made to territory on the southern side. Why, undoubtedly, wise and skilful public men, having an object to accomplish, may take advantage of occasions. Indian wars are an occasion; a fear of the occupation of Texas by the British was an occasion; but when the occasion came, under the pressure of which, or under the justification of which the thing could be done, it was done, and done skilfully. Let me say one thing further; and that is, that if slavery were abolished, as it was supposed to have been, throughout all Mexico, before the revolution and the establishment of the Texan government, then, if it were desirable to have possession of Texas by purchase, as a means of preventing its becoming a British possession, I suppose that object could have been secured by making it a free territory of the United States, as well as a slave territory.

Sir, in my great desire not to prolong this debate, I have omitted what I intended to say on a particular question under the motion of the honorable senator from Missouri, proposing an amendment to the resolution of the honorable member from Illinois; and that is, upon the propriety and expediency of admitting California, under all circumstances, just as she is. The more general subjects involved in this question are now before the Senate under the resolutions of the honorable member from Kentucky. I will say that I feel under great obligations to that honorable member for introducing the subject, and for the very lucid speech which he made, and which has been so much read throughout the whole country. I am also under great obligations to the honorable member from Tennessee, for the light which he has shed upon this subject; and, in some respects, it will be seen that I differ very little from the leading subjects submitted by either of those honorable gentlemen.

Now, sir, when the direct question of the admission of California shall be before the Senate, I propose — but not before every other gentleman who has a wish to address the Senate shall have gratified that desire — to say something upon the boundaries of California, upon the constitution of California, and upon the expediency, under all the circumstances, of admitting her with that constitution.

Mr. CALHOUN. One word, and I have done; and that word is, that, notwithstanding the acquisition of the vast territory of Texas represented by the senator from Massachusetts, it is the fact that all that addition to our territory made it by no means equal to what the Northern States had excluded us from before that acquisition. The territory lying west between the Mississippi and the Rocky Mountains is three fourths of the whole of Louisiana; and that which lies between the Mississippi and the Ohio, added to that, makes a much greater extent of territory than Florida, and Texas, and that portion of Louisiana that has fallen to our share.

Mr. Walker moved the postponement of the further consideration of the resolutions until to-morrow, which was agreed to.

THE END.